READING BETWEEN THE RHYMES

A RHYMING SYMPHONY OF THOUGHTS

GIRIDHAR JADED

ARPress

ARPress
45 Dan Road Suite 36
Canton MA 02021

Hotline: 1(800) 220-7660
Fax: 1(855) 752-6001

Ordering Information:
Quantity sales. Special discounts are available on quantity purchases by corporations, associations, and others. For details, contact the publisher at the address above.

Printed in the United States of America.

ISBN-13:   Paperback   979-8-89389-916-0
           eBook   979-8-89389-917-7

Library of Congress Control Number: 2024923846

The way to one's dreams is often times a hard fought one,
At times needing one to stand apart, on pedestals one's own,
And to stand alone is hard, easier if there are
ones who believe in your sojourn,
For it's belief & hope that life thrives on, & grows along,
To have someone who believes in you more than you at times,
Can be the difference in marching along inch by inch, mile by mile,
A thank you to my Sister & brother for believing in my Art,
For a subtle belief as well can end up playing a bigger part,
And to the one who believes more, stands by
me during every step of this journey,
Even my rhyming words fall short to thank you, my lovely Wifey.

Contents

When fear creeps

Virulent are the waters that are deep,
Where fear demons of all sizes and shapes creep,
Some frail-some looking, rather weak,
Some monstrous, intimidating, looking hungry for weeks.
The journey of life, it tends to pass through,
Some silent waters and at times raging ones too,
And when those mystic currents really get wild,
It's not uncommon to lose one's mind,
And to lose one's way in a cosmic spiral storm,
That brews in one's own mind, making you feel outside the norm.
To then occasionally becomes necessary this fight,
For otherwise, the dreams you truly believe in, would not take flight.
Fear is a demon, worthy of a battle, and fulfilling when conquered,
The best view of this demon is with its facial geographies scattered.
What's thy fear? What is it in you, needing a beating?
Fight it once, fight it again, for winning those battles is quite a feeling.

—————————————Downpourofwords

Footnote: *List down the top 10 fears in your life. You may keep it a secret. But as you start to pen those down, a few of them vanish by themselves. As if they were non-existent to begin with. The rest, when you stare down in a moment of acceptance, shall start to seem smaller & smaller, with time. And there's a hidden pleasure in conquering your fear demons.*

Walk with me?

Will you walk with me to a place?
Where we shall both revel, amidst some solace,
Maybe lie down a little, on nature's bed or sit upright,
To wait it out, to then gaze at stars of the night.
As we settle into a breathing rhythm,
I'll play a song that you love to listen,
And once the final notes do meticulously subside,
Let me and you drift into an elegant, deftly slide,
Into a realm where only me and you shall preside,
Resting our buttocks, holding hands, side by side,
And in those moments lived on that blank space,
There won't be a rush oh, not even a trace.
I think I know a place like that, and it's in my mind,
It's perfect for nothingness, playfulness and to unwind.
————————————————————Downpourofwords

Footnote: *At times, the rides we can go on in our magical minds, are more heartfelt than the realities of the worldly kind. Spare a thought for what could be possible if two totally different minds met at a place bereft of the realities of the humankind!*

Blinking eyes

Aren't all of us lonely in some little way,
Feeling whole a while, then losing our way,
For life's short but rather long as well,
Tossing twists, riveting turns it continues to dispel.
And it's not easy for there are barely other human ropes to grope,
For loneliness manifests from being left alone to cope.
And filling that void, needs you in a rather rigorous role,
Often wondering if it's the birth of an irksome mole,
That could grow and engulf a lively soul,
By dispelling it into the loneliness abode.
Where there's darkness that lurks at every single blink,
And those frivolous feelings run amok, up until that ugly brink,
Where every passing soul is an enemy, including oneself,
Those moments in life are best left, as unfelt,
Whilst out on a patrol one silent night, I see many such blinking eyes,
Each waiting a turn, to fight and get back to the light.
——————————————————Downpourofwords

Footnote: *In an age where togetherness is measured by the frequency of technological connect instead of an emotional connect, it is not uncommon to find lonely souls, being lonely in silence. All the answers to the togetherness you seek, reside within you.*

That soulful trance

The stage was set, and the lights were warm,
There was no music, but the crowd cheered on,
The leather jackets, they glistened in the night,
A million flashing phones, and an empty stage in sight.
Some had come there, to check a box,
In a bucket list believed to unlock life's locks,
Whilst some were there for their BFF was going,
And a day alone binge watching, strangely seemed boring.
Some were there for the pure bliss that music brings,
Ready to dispel in music, to create a memory that clings.
Some were there to see in pure form and flesh,
What makes an Artist standout from the rest?
And that's when the arena erupts into life,
From music that played in every car and then came the blinding lights,
And the tears also cry, as a voice comes out,
Creating a soulful trance over whistles, screams and wilder shouts.
—————————————Downpourofwords

Footnote: *The reasons for which we indulge in something, end up defining us as a human being. The more those moments that you really did something, for you wanted that ethereal feeling, the more fulfilling shall life be, besides all the show and tell we falsely believe in.*

A little elf

As the night traversed in pin drop silence,
Every moment felt like a stifling penance,
From all but missing of a blissful presence,
Of someone wanted in every known sense.
In drifting in a feeling that's still a mystery to science,
Floating waywardly in a maze of confusing signs,
But one's soul though, often erupts into a dance,
With stomping feet making the Earth shake, and do so in a trance,
Dancing to a mysterious tune, aided by seductive, hypnotic voices,
Listening to which brings déjà vu of a few heartfelt times.
And whilst swaying to that trance, on a silent night,
Even a red light from a switched off TV seems like twilight,
The night called out, on a feeling deep down inside,
A yearning to be with that someone, even if a little while,
That someone is a part of my own self,
A believer of a person, a playful, battler of a little elf.
——————————————————Downpourofwords

Footnote: *Missing someone is quite common. How often do you miss the real you, the you that only you know, is YOU? Do you feel a craving more intense than a craving for someone, or is it a rather mild one?*

That downward slide

In a playful mood, whilst on a joyful ride,
I once went along, on a surging tide,
And it's on that ride that I realized,
To feel that much awaited tingle, I had to rise,
First higher up, and then make a downward glide,
Braving a few spaces where those fears reside.
Rise higher at first so the worldly human crabs subside,
Trying hard to silence that part of me, where my dreams reside,
I start by nipping them off, then place them side by side,
But it was too many to deal with, and I ain't one to hide,
So, I took a leap of faith, into that rising tide,
Until the horizon was new and I saw falcons, not masks or hides,
And when the sight of my horizon was cemented my mind,
I felt the thinning air, an absolute rush, one of its kind.
And once on a higher pedestal in sync with my mind,
I knew I had to plunge, deep inside, on a downward slide,
And down I went, forever feeling the wind in my hair,
And conquering those decade long fears, it just seemed fair,
And now I have a frail-some yet sweet memory dangling in the air,
One I can pluck and replay in my minds lair,
To replay my downward slide, away from
haters, the envious and those glares,
And then those unlived moments and dreams in me, that were at war,
With myself more than anyone else, seemed long gone, by and far.

—Downpourofwords

Footnote: *Doing things we like, is like flying an imaginary kite. A kite which doesn't need a thread to be high, so long as there's someone in you who likes to try. And to do so, not caring about the ones dry, meant to pry, needs a dive deep down like a blinding slide.*

Conundrum of sorts

Often-times, in the frailties of a human mind,
Dwells a species, its ancient, one of a kind,
One that evolved though with the sands of time,
Evolving with insights, getting better all the while,
Formless, yet omnipresent, and filled with sheer might,
Prevalent in its presence yet living comfortably out of sight.
It's this species that really does define,
The way forward and the count of heartfelt smiles,
From oneself and with the ones we meet on this ride,
In what we call as a whimsical journey named life.
The species it controls even the legacies we leave behind.
It's something that drives one and all, uniquely through our minds.
The existence of what we call as them simmering THOUGHTS,
Living with them every moment yet never seeing
them, is more a conundrum of sorts,
And without the thoughts, wouldn't we be zombies on war bound carts?
For life and even death would feel lame, amidst all those flying darts.
—————————————————Downpourofwords

Footnote: *Conundrum – a confusing or difficult question or a problem. Who are we without our thoughts? What sets us humans apart are our thoughts, be it the ones that prick us like darts or the ones that light up the magical sparks. If mindfulness is being aware of our most intrinsic thoughts, hopelessness is living life without being aware of our thoughts.*

Comfortably Inside

On a certain lazy Saturday afternoon,
When the bones seem to be melting on their own,
And being lazy in a way, induces that soulful calm,
In the comfort of the A/C that's constantly on,
I went for a walk in the afternoon sun,
And it started off being a little fun,
Before the heat slowly started to seep in,
Well before I was about welcome my newfound fling,
To get a few paces, to hear my heartbeat thumping,
And to feel the nerves widen, from the blood pumping.
The sweat drops from the run, seemed to be calming my skin down,
That's when I noticed a worrisome looking man, mowing that green lawn.
It made me wonder about the wonderful choice I ride,
To be out there in the Sun for a run or be comfortably inside.
————————————————Downpourofwords

Footnote: *An avoidable discomfort for me (being out in the summer sun), is a necessity for an innocent family. A moment of unacknowledged comfort for me (comfort of our homes), is a leisure someone else craves silently.*

Out, again

I think I had come to a forceful stop,
Having pushed myself into a shady little spot,
But then I saw where I had set my sights,
Was to be long drawn and needed some fight.
So, I straddled along once again this time,
Hoping to hang around, a little longer this time,
For if I have found myself keeping a count of the times,
That I have fallen, having taken jibes,
Jibes from no one else but my own frivolous little mind,
It plays tantrums of its very own kind.
My mind at times, is a statistical maze,
Often leaves me reeling, in a dreary haze,
And it's in such times, I let things go to a standstill,
Very much so, against my own will.
And to be out in the open for a lonesome walk,
Is a way to get my thoughts and my mind to talk,
To be in the dark a while is ok, but I head out once again,
Trying to not let go, not let it all go in vain.
————————————————Downpourofwords

Footnote: *Lethargy is an enemy that invades us slowly. A simple act of taking some walks at times, can be a way out of life's anomalies.*

Comodo dragon

Like vultures in the sky hovering above,
Drudgery hovers in life, with a deadly alibi, on the move,
It sprays a scent that slowly kills a human's inner need,
To be engaged in any activity or for that matter a welcome deed.
It engulfs the mind that's forever wants to fly,
But chained by its alibi, a comodo dragon hanging tight,
And slowly the dragon through its wickedly guile,
Transfers its ugly layers onto the innocent mind, the imbecile,
Soon turning into layers of fat and wrinkles on the skin,
Along with allergies, diseases with symptoms as its kith & kin.
The deadly vice of this dragon is hard to break,
But wellness is from those irksome steps, often hard to take,
Drudgery and it's comodo dragon are scared only of action,
Can be beaten though, with an ounce of resilient gumption.
—————————————————Downpourofwords

Footnote: *In today's world, technology is like a comodo dragon
that hangs to us real tight, making us constantly lose sight, of what's
right. To be working out a little, to be out in that sunlight. Takes
a lot to tame one's mind, to live a life feeling bodily alright.*

Cocoon, big or small

I often have a love-hate affair with books, from long back
Those books once reminded me of a heavy sack,
That I was bound to carry no matter what,
To keep learning the *'what, how, where and why'* on the trot.
Every year, the lessons grew, into something new,
The real moments of being blown away, a paltry few,
It's didn't make sense then, but it does fully now,
As an adult mind makes sense of the why, and the how.
For if I couldn't make sense of the things around,
I would be trapped in a cocoon of my own,
And sitting inside, I think I wouldn't want to wander,
For the world outside is cruel, & there's lightning and thunder,
I have used books & wisdom to expand my cocoon,
Oftentimes being amazed at possibilities, at
times even landing on the moon.

—————————————————Downpourofwords

Footnote: *Books are and will always be our passage to a better realm. A way from darkness to light, a way from being stagnant in life to feeling alive, a way to know more and to grow more, is possible only if there's a constant camaraderie in life, with books.*

Lost Charm?

Somewhere in my childhood, years ago,
When I was in school, trying my best to know,
As to why is it, I had to study so much on how,
For those numbers, dates seemed to land some hefty blows.
But words were different, they lent me a serene essence,
Which would leave behind its lingering presence,
Of a world that existed around, yet wasn't seen,
With endless possibilities, that remain vastly unseen,
And somewhere back then I also did realize,
That words could be with played and organized,
My wordplay even has a name, its known as 'Poetry',
Where rhythmic words dance along, with a soulful sanctity.
I read about Poetry and learnt about the imagery,
And also, about phonetics, intrigue & that mystery.
Now I wonder if Poetry has over the ages lost its charm,
What could I do to bring it back to where it belongs?
——————————————————————Downpourofwords

Footnote: *Poetry fosters perception enhancement, helps to engage the mind, and thought formulation that leads to working our brains. We do not engage our brains much when we binge watch. Unless we mind constantly processes what's occurring on the screen into multiple possibilities. The times that it occurs are rare & limited to moments when we relate an on-screen event to our lives, from the past, present or future. Reading Poetry needs a mind to read, make sense, try to understand the thought, a message, the possibilities & the imagery if any. An artform to enhance our minds, await to revive its destiny.*

Crazy train

I wished for my life to be a crazy train,
With open windows, & secretly welcomed untimely rains,
That would pour every now and then, to then be washing away,
At the drain from life & the numbing pain from those gloomy days.
I used to see those tracks, though blurry & distant,
Egging me on to make a sideways hop, but I was hesitant,
Maybe from being caught up in my mind, in ways too deep,
Or from obligations from life that are for ours to forever keep.
It's in things that we let go stagnant, that lethargy breeds,
Lethargy rules most part of our lives yet intent gives it the creeps.
I loitered along, resurrected a few crumbling bridges,
I could have easily hopped on out, but against life, who keeps grudges?
But then I saw that bridge, saw clearly, I couldn't
fathom a life spent being vane,
And I found my crazy train & my thoughts falling like untimely rains,
To keep pouring my heart out, to be a Downpour of words,
And soon I saw my words grow mightier than them swords.

——————————————————Downpourofwords

Footnote: *There's a hidden bliss in engaging in things that we are passionate about. What's the name of your crazy train? Writing is mine.*

Counting them flashes

What difference does it make I wonder?
If life hands it all to us on a lavish platter,
For then all that is left to do, to keep running helter-skelter,
Changing lanes between life & its materialistic pleasures,
How long would those Agera RS talks feel exciting like ghosts?
Or those invites to a party from a celebrity host,
How many days would we shop till we drop?
How often shall we keep travelling on the trot?
Wouldn't life be living being an exhibition of sorts?
That shines in all its grandeur like a golden field full of corns.
In being that ear to a heart writhing in pain,
Or in being a cupped hand for a tear that's shed in pain,
Or for that matter, in making an aching heart flutter,
Or to chase one's dreams like 'nothing else matters',
A life lived only for the gold rush, is a treachery path,
Like caught in circles, counting them flashes in the dark.
————————————Downpourofwords

Footnote: *Is life a lot about showing off? Or also about finding a way to play our part? What we seek shall also define where we land. On a firm footing called Destiny, or the treacherous material quick sands?*

Destiny Offline

I thought I had nailed that piece of code,
That skimmed through millions of maze-like rows,
Of gibberish that made the chat room work
I even tried to write up my own source code,
What I was after, was a chat with destiny,
I had tried chatting in the real world & found it to be slippery.
For many of the roads I took, led me nowhere,
Or got misled by my own mind, & questions filled the air.
I cracked the login and went through the maze, in a fright,
Where all I did for a while was to swipe left and right,
And after a while it seemed as if I had cracked it,
For there was a flash of a bright blinding light.
I typed a hello & a smiley, beaming with hope inside,
A popup flew onto my screen, it read 'Destiny Offline'.
—————————————————————Downpourofwords

Footnote: *We all ponder about that uncertainty named destiny. What are we here to do? What is it that I can do that's my best? Where will I be one day, where is it that I want to be. Unfortunately, there's no technology to have a conversation to find the answers. But the login & password are unique to each one of us, and inside our mind.*

A Daydream

One day I found myself standing tall on a stage,
Holding a guitar, strumming it seemed, in a rage,
Standing in the back I was, the front belonged to the singer,
Who had mastered the act of stealing the thunder?
I seemed happy to be holding a playback guitar,
For it to resonate back, only for me to hear.
I did strum along, following the chords of a song,
Sung by a Rockstar but those words were my own.
In being there, and hearing those raucous cheers,
I hate to cry but who can hold back the tears?
I was being a silent spectator out there,
Feeling a creation of mine fill the void & the nightly air.
And that's when I hear the Rocky Balboa theme play,
It's my alarm that shook me up, & I welcomed the morning rays.
—————————————————Downpourofwords

Footnote: *We can be anything we want in our dreams. There's also a hidden bliss in the plain act of dreaming & when actions start aligning to those dreams, is when it feels worth to start believing.*

Create your own juggernaut

A rolling ball is what it is, a juggernaut called life,
Won't stop if we let it roll, can do so tirelessly all the while,
Until the time that it's halted right in its tracks,
From a willing mind, trying to wrest control off its pangs,
To try and steer it to a nicer, quieter place,
Where dreams can be probed deeper, in some solace.
And to then wrap as paper planes in a glistening paper,
To let them fly high, where the stars play poker.
But the juggernaut won't stop, and it never will,
There's no point trying to bring it to a standstill.
The best we can do is to make some moments our own,
And create a juggernaut of such moments we call as our own,
For despite all of life's stumbles along the way,
Being even an inch closer to our dreams, is still a victory any given day.
————————————————Downpourofwords

Footnote: *Life will never be kind enough to hand us moments of perfection. Life will be life. An endless charade of events that seem to occur no matter what. Every one of us has the same 24 hours yet the ones who manage to create their own juggernaut of moments of rightful intent, go onto achieve what they truly deserve.*

A 1000-year stopwatch

If a timer is set from now to 1000 years,
For the world to end for sure, with no sense of a fear,
What do you think we would change?
To let nine generations experience life, in all its range,
To leave behind a world where it's still ok to breathe,
Breathe air from the open, not through pipes with unease,
To have enough water for everyone's basic needs,
And healthy food for the innocent bellies to feed,
Would we care about the animals about to go extinct?
Or would we rely on 4K images from now, as a quick fix?
What would we do to help the generations thrive?
What would we leave as rightful lessons left behind?
Would we have neatly wrapped answers for them to see & smile,
Or would we live as we do today, for after death, who'd be here to whine?
Maybe it's time all nations agree on such a reverse timer,
And re-engineer our future to leave behind a better world order.

——————————————————Downpourofwords

Footnote: *We all have examples of imposing imaginary deadlines on our minds, to achieve certain goals in life. We call these as milestones & we apply them to studying, tasks, chores, necessities of life. Is it time to set certain milestones for the lives yet to step onto this world?*

Lessons of heritage

Of all the lessons learnt from heritage,
Which ones you think, are your favorites?
For what we carry over does pave the way,
To a future in which we shall have a say,
For the rest is unto unrelenting human brilliance,
Forever bent on making our lives more convenient,
At costs which we shall one day, repent,
But whoever listened to a thought filled Poet who vents?
For in a need to blindly invent and reinvent,
Can lie an alluring cascade, for later to repent,
The lessons passed on over generations,
They are a way of capturing pure human essence,
Into the itsy-bitsy gestures or habits that make sense,
To become a part of us as we grow our presence,
I go through these thoughts, as I iron a wrinkled shirt,
For it was from Dad, that I learned how to do it first.
And that's when I see an ad flashing at me in the eye,
Of a machine that washes, dries and tidies up & irons clothes, and I sigh.
————————————————————————Downpourofwords

Footnote: *When the dust settles on our worldly presence, what lingers behind is only our essence. In the minds of the ones we touched in our lives, even the ones who were never on our side. In such an endless cycle called life, what's worthy of passing on is the essence from our heritage and the tidbits of lessons we learned, from having been passed along.*

Names on the Seashore

Living a life without a well-defined purpose,
Is more akin to heeding to innumerable "I suppose",
Or like writing your name on the sands close to the sea,
Where your presence is as limited as every wave that recedes,
For in writing your name on the tumultuous sands on the beach,
Defines the realms that you shall reach,
For the waves are unstoppable, not meant to empathize,
On the beauty that you left behind, on the seaside,
And with every wave that grows stronger with the falling Sun,
Your name shall be erased, watching it happen, is no fun,
Isn't life, like this more often? That's a haunting question,
That resides in us, and accompanies us till oblivion?
For what we try to do in that moment of stupidity,
Is to try and leave a mark in something that's meant to be temporary,
It's totally alright to do that for in that moment lies a victory,
Of seeing oneself like never, despite being temporary,
But if that moment starts to define our life, as our destiny,
A life lived like that, sooner or later becomes an anomaly.
Go ahead, write your life like it was meant to be a mystery,
One to be looked upon with hope, on an upward trajectory.

—————————————Downpourofwords

Footnote: *No one else can be blamed for who we are, today. No one
else can be blamed for who will be, one day. Of course the life path
one takes can be altered and in significant ways by the ones around us,
but to let those deviations hinder you, or to power you on to surge with
more vigor, lies completely in your hands, and more so in our minds.*

Motherhood

I was once at a seashore like I always wanted to be,
Watching the seagulls and the white sands, with my lovely wife, with me,
And while there, I had to deal with my own fallacies,
For even if the sands were warm, bereft of human tomfoolery,
The waters were a bit cold, for the season was Wintery,
Yet the Sun had his say, made it feel like a beautiful symphony,
By being the warmth that the wandering souls needed,
To take that fleeting chance, like an opportunity badly needed,
To feel warm on the Seaside in the month of December,
To try and create moments that are worthy, to be remembered,
That's when I saw a mother and her Son walk into the waters,
Like the cold and the chills ceased to matter,
And in the next few minutes that trespassed in the sea breeze,
I felt a part of me take notice, and humbly freeze,
For the son and his Dad knew the truth, the waters were cold,
But the Mother in her was a Mother, meant to be bold.
She went ahead, leading her family like a wolfpack,
Knowing that those nimble steps shall follow, behind her back,
And she went into the waters, took that much wanted dip,
And soon enough her family had a moment, wanting to enjoy the trip,
A beautiful lesson it transpired in a few moments so deep,
A mother would cross them barriers, not one to meekly weep,
I thank myself for having been there in that moment,
Some pleasures in life worthy of being watched,
with nothing else to lament.
—————————————Giridhar Jaded

Footnote: *Life is full of observations, if our eyes and minds are open and acceptant to see. I have always been fascinated by the lengths that Motherhood will go to ensure the wellbeing of an offspring. From knowing that a cat sometimes devours one of its own, knowing it's her own, to be able to survive for the rest of her offspring, to seeing a mother give away her life & dreams to see the dreams of her little ones flourish, life is full of examples of the pure Love that Motherhood upholds. This poem was penned while watching a family of four play by the beachside in Panama City beach, Florida.*

Who am I?

Watching a Pet (Dog) and its owners have their moment at a beach,
Is sometimes worthy, more like nailing a peach,
For in the act of being a master & a prodigy,
There is a camaraderie, unfolding like a soulful mystery,
As I watch the dog leap around, happily playing snatch,
I realize a moment of humankind, usually hard to catch,
Hard to catch not from being bestowed the ability to realize,
But usually from being caught up, in a need to materialize.
What I see is a humble need on part of the Dog to try & dissipate,
A truth we all know as unexplainable, hard to imitate,
For the Dog isn't stupid to begin with, to keep playing fetch,
Every time you throw the ball far, for it to run & fetch,
For its not so much about the act of playing fetch,
But in being with you as someone who would do everything to forget,
The world around, in order to make his/her presence felt,
That the Pet sees himself/herself in a moment hard to regret,
And he/she knows that there's a moment of joy in you, that you feel,
Whenever he does a trick, or plainly ever so humbly kneels.
And in that feeling of pleasing the hell out of you,
The Dog displays a sense of belonging, inhumane, something new.
If he/she had the intellect to sit along, & retrospect,
The Dog would have sat by your side, probably inspect,
The fallacies of the human mind, not to forget,
But being a soulful being that it is, a Dog chooses, to just forget,
Forget one's own discomfort and everything else to worry about,

In being your companion, doesn't matter if walking on out,
Into unchartered territories or the cold beach that we ourselves would not,
For in being a human being's buddy, it sees a reason, blissful & stout,
That it belies everything else & hangs on around,
Like a soulmate who's hard to ignore, to be pushed around,
Such moments in life are worth the realizations they bring along,
Pets are a means to feel alive in everything
else, that's mostly seems wrong.
———————————————————Downpourofwords

Footnote: *We often take the unconditional love from our Pets for granted. With a side argument weighing heavy in our minds that they do not have intellect, like we do. But in hindsight, a pet might be going to great lengths at appeasing us, for it loves the way our faces light up at certain acts of hers or his.*

Like a fighter

In those moments when the minds wander,
Into spaces where your Earth shudders,
And you feel engulfed in silent tremors,
Emanating from the inside, in silent waters,
When you feel like running away somewhere,
Running wild like you really don't care,
Heading straight into an abyss down under,
Or to be picking up a fight, with that violent thunder,
There's only one thing that's key to remember,
When was the last time you felt this tremor?
And with it behind & you ahead in time, did it still instill a shiver?
For you came out alright then, like a fighter,
Hang in there, just a little while longer,
Life has its lows but also happiness around the corner,
If you wiped off the sweat once, you can once again,
Being alright feels much better, after the pain.

———————————————Downpourofwords

Footnote: *The worst moments that we have been, can also lead the way, to a bright future yet unseen. Experiences that we carry, even when of the forgettable kind, can help put things into perspective, to move forward, minus the worries.*

Stone story

A lonely stone somewhere on the road,
Had a surprisingly striking story to be told,
For what it had witnessed in two incidences,
Were legions apart and bereft of coincidences.
For one fine day, years ago at the same time,
A stone had been a weapon behind a crime,
For its strength had been used to infuse a permanent mime,
Onto someone who until then had had a brimming life,
Was even learning to win, against life & its strife.
And now the stone lay here this day, a few feet away,
The blood and its traces are long gone, been washed away,
But nature has mystical ways of keeping things in the fray,
At times with an anticlimax, blowing people's minds away,
The stone had to come face to face again, with crime,
This time held up and thrown right on time, on the right kind,
Against a man who had killed many, of his own kind,
After shooting innocent strangers singing & dancing, looking to unwind,
While one was the story of a mixed-up emotion,
The other was a testimony to a toxic emotional concoction,
The stone became a part in some way, of righting a wrong,
But to the ones who passed, what fault was it of their own?
————————————————Downpourofwords

Footnote: *Events and incidents will continue to occur for as long as there is time, and as long as there is life & strife. It's not the people who flare up and act imbecile that suffer, for they already do in a way. It's those million moments of silent sufferings that occur from the ones left behind, to relive it again and again, in their minds.*

Lightning behind the dark clouds

If all the ashes from the bodies were swept,
Swiftly under a dark blanket named death,
From different places, ages, the ones who recently died,
Some being missed in abundance, some with no tears shed,
If those ashes were to gather into a monstrous cloud,
A cloud thick and black, and looking menacingly cold,
With blinding flashes, seen across thousands of miles,
Flashes from moments lived well, the moments sublime,
From all those lives that had now bid their time,
And in seeing faces form from the flashes, even with a smile,
Would you recognize a smiling face flashing by?
Summoned by nature, to just see you smile,
Would you admire & applaud that flash, for a little while?
For then that flash in the ash would feel worthwhile.
Even a face that never had many heartfelt smiles,
Not from loved ones, not from strangers alike, when alive,
Can find an acceptance after having died,
While some find an acceptance while alive, & after having died.
Memories are what make all the lives worthwhile,
And I see a lightning, & another cloud of ash vanish away in time.

——————————————Downpourofwords

Footnote: *An imaginary rendition of a thought that that ones that recently departed this abode, make a final attempt at being seen for what they were, and for moments that they felt most alive.*

Just a few things I want

I want to swim in the blue lagoons,
I want to sing with the wild Baboons,
I want to fly with the sea Vultures,
I want to bask under ancient scriptures,
I want to ride on the back of Dolphins,
I want my mind to be a constant tailspin,
I want to dive deep into those craters,
I want to sit in peace with Alligators,
I want to dispel myself into the dark,
I want to jump out with demons on my back,
I want to soar into possibilities unlike,
I want to dispel notions into the dark,
I want to slide into those spaces in time,
Where impossible is a dismissible fallacy of the mind.
————————————————Downpourofwords

Footnote: *Careless, uninhibited and harmless thoughts are also a gift in life.*

Morning sun

One day, the sun shall sneak right in,
Through those curtains, and keep on shining,
And reach my eyes in a way, like never before,
Waking me a little yet waking me some more.
I shall open my lazy eyes with a smile,
For on such mornings, I can have my say on time,
Not be too worried on scurrying around,
About a commute rather short, yet one that seemed long,
What goes around does come around,
I shall wait for the blissful morning to come along.

A few times I have basked in its heartfelt warmth,
Inside my mind though, and it has played a part,
For if you daydream enough, it will be enough,
To lead eventually into actions, to get out of the rough,
And until that morning comes, I shall carry along,
Doing what's necessary, to be playing along,
And when the day arrives, I shall head for a walk,
No tea or coffee or a puff, I shall plainly walk,
And when I return, I know it wasn't something I had planned,
Yet having a smile on my face on how it panned.

—————————————Downpourofwords

Footnote: *Every writer's daydream in a way is waking up to not be heading for a day job, or at least for some days.*

Why to fit in?

You told me once that I don't fit in,
And in my dictionary, the phrase 'fit in' doesn't fit in,
Yet I am glad you told me, because now I think I know,
Why did it matter to you then, and even now?
For it showed that the 4K vision of your eyes,
Was funneled by content streamed with lies,
And what you saw and what you heard,
Made a home in your heart, word by word,
For what you could stream is just a tiny part,
Of an ocean that I am, filled with a million parts.
And I do this, not with an intention to hide,
But deep within me are highs & shallows, unfathomable to confide,
And yet in my life, in your eyes, I am to constantly smile & glide,
Seated in the front row, wearing a forever smile.
When you move on, I won't blame you for walking your mile,
I shall wish you a Goodbye, this time with a genuine smile,
Hoping that it would find a place even in your naked miles,
If life's a game, I won't give up on my heartfelt tries,
Your version of a fit in, is not how I choose to ride my ride.
And what I let you see, by peeking inside,
Were ripples on a river, not the vibrant tides,
And while you are lost in trying to just fit in,
Caught up even in illustrious moments, not ones felt deep within,
All I ask from you is to go on, with all you got,
But what solace do you find, in trying to find me a spot,
Into a place where I don't believe I even belong?
I hope one day you fit in just perfect, and I will be long gone.
————————————Downpourofwords

Footnote: *In a world where there are more heartbreaks*
than there are heartfelt heartaches from missing someone,
a breakup poem with a positive tone fits right in.

Hang on tight

In those fast paced so called moments,
Forced upon by life, like gushing torrents,
Where sanity often goes for a toss, in silence,
Not questioning life's madness, nor its presence,
And breathing seems like a chore, unrelenting,
Just hold on a little more, there's always something coming.
But how do you know for sure if it's coming?
A good question, but the start must be with believing.
For without a belief, there can't be a reason,
And with mere belief too, boulders can't be broken,
To not believe is an unforgiving crime,
And so is believing and idling, whiling away time.
If you put in your steps to whatever it is that shines,
Deep inside your heart, that thing which brings you soulful smiles,
Be rest assured that what's happening also has an ending,
And like I said, there's always something better coming.
But life's a game, and it loves to keep you busy,
It smiles back at you, knowing you know it won't be easy.
What life throws versus what makes you feel your flow,
A balance of the two is needed for if not, the dreams get outgrown.
Truth be told, the pace of life is a mystery created by us,
Calling it a mystery, a façade that comfortably comforts,
Drift through life like a lonesome fly or tearing
into air, like a hummingbird,
The choice is YOURS, its true alphabet by alphabet, word by word.
Whatever be your story, believe, remember to flap your wings,
Occasionally for your dreams, not just to life's feisty winds.

——————————————Downpourofwords

Footnote: *To believe is human. To not believe as well, is human.*
To once have believed, and to forego that belief is also human.

So stark

I think you have known it all along,
That we might not have our own parting song,
All it would be, would be walking on,
For something that wasn't, could never be wrong?
The inklings though, have always been there,
And in the end, it's only seems fair,
For we did walk along, even if just a while,
Under the same beating sun, we made it worth our while.
And in all this while, amidst the smiles & even turmoil,
What's been burning at both ends, is a certain midnight oil,
Burnt inside one, whilst diffusing scent in the other,
Like a scented feather flying across, when two hearts carelessly flutter.
Whatever was felt, also brought along moments sublime,
We said our cheers, what if we never had that wine.
And now I know that the days that we together walked,
Seem like pleasant dreams, & also as nightmares, seeming so stark.
————————————————————Downpourofwords

Footnote: *To feel the ultimate high and an abysmal
low, cannot be felt anywhere else, but in Love.*

The art of falling apart

Across all the centuries that humans have evolved
How many a notion have been dissolved?
Perplexing too are the ways in which we have evolved,
Stranger are those million boundaries we have crossed.

From dreaming to fly one day to now flying for dreams,
From living to survive to challenging death in its own realms,
From sleeping in caves to sleeping on a bed that behaves,
From eating raw protein to extracting strands of casein.

One such evolution is the Art of falling apart,
In situations in life, that are dramatically stark,
Dramatic, with due respect to hardships that come along,
But what justifies magnifying reactions, to problems rather small?

For just like being stuck in an elevator, and the incumbent fear,
Cannot be compared to being chased by a grizzly bear,
Yet we have evolved in the act of magnifying our fears,
To find a pretext to be known as one shedding tears,

For if it is inevitable in life to not fall apart,
It is in our realms, how well do we play a part,
A part to be played meticulously like a skillful craftsman at drunk in his art,
Doesn't matter if it's a loss or rather from a broken heart,
It's not fully our fault for the seeds were sown generations ago,
Looking busy, handling stress as acceptant parts, hard to forego.

Yet there is a hope if we look on our insides, more,
To try and dispel our heart and our mind, into that core,
Call it yoga, meditation, breathing or mindfulness to go,
The evolution of the future is inside, not in the places we go.
——————————————————Downpourofwords

Footnote: *The answers are within you. To someone reeling in the depths, those words might seem to be bee-shit. But the truth of the matter is that it's true.*

Quote - Diamond untouched

You could be that diamond that I can never hold in my hands,
Yet I smile, having seen your deepest shimmer, in a way no one else can.

Quote - Hyperventilating

Don't we all hyperventilate from not doing things, necessary?
To be moving on in life, more like accessories?
There is peace though, in knowing we have company,
There is pride though, in acting upon it incessantly.

Quote - live life a better way?

I don't think you can allow yourself to have an off day,
Until you see yourself making some headway,
For if not, like a million others-you shall be lost, in trying to find a way,
To one day sit & wonder, I should have lived life in a better way.

A wake-up call

He walked tall, like a raging fireball,
Burning in an un-been desire, he'd seen it all,
He had a sprint, like there is nowhere to fall,
He stomped on adversity, like a cannon ball,
He tightened loose ends like he knew it all,
Even made sense in broken paintings on those seeping walls.
He crisscrossed mountains, be it in spring or fall,
He hopped across the oceans, often leaping high and tall,
He rode the waves of authority, like a general,
He stomped on resistance, he made it look trivial.
He followed in footsteps of some who were long gone,
Used them lessons, to create his own hopeful song,
He loved in abundance, often bared it all,
He lived more in silence, observing and feeling it all,
Then the calm in his inner self, got broken by an alarm,
And he woke up, found himself by the bed, having taken a fall.

—————————————————Downpourofwords

Footnote: *Are some dreams a reflection of something deeper? What if we dream for a reason, even if we tend to remember only parts of our entire night's dreams?*

A choice so hard

It was a hard choice that she had to make,
To try and decide between the real and fake,
What lay ahead as always, was unique,
Filled with an unnerving lure, and that mystique,
The hunger for Love, doesn't it drive us all,
At times taking us to the skies or plummeting to a crashing fall?
At times from seeing someone in Love, and smiling,
Or from seeing a gesture of love, with feelings?
And she was someone who had seen it all,
Had waded across turbulent waters, and had walked tall,
A look into a future, with promises and Love,
Often took her into her past, memories as fresh as clove,
And in running from those places and memories,
Seemed to turn calendars into a blur, filled with drudgery,
And there he was, another charmer with that mystery,
Carrying along a handsome serving of good old flattery,
She sat in silence, closed her eyes, and sighed,
It was a moment she yearned eternally, but silently cried.

———————————————————Downpourofwords

Footnote: *To fall madly in love is a wish that many have, yet in the beaches of Love, many get hurt often, whilst acting naive.*

My soulful song

The thoughts that mess up my mind,
Are also the ones keeping me alive,
For in them, I do not see a strife,
And I welcome them as a way of life.
And in the hunger for being alive,
I shall try making it a worthwhile ride,
And I shall rip open facets that hide,
To dive deep and see what's inside,
For only then would my crazy mind,
Subtly find a peaceful way to unwind.
But right now, I ain't got that time,
I have a few pertinent answers to go find,
I shall let the buzz live on, for I'll battle on,
Till the day that I carve out my own soulful song.

————————————————————Downpourofwords

Footnote: *What is life without a few unanswered questions, without a few unconquered demons, without a few rightful reasons?*

A childhood game

At some point in my childhood,
When I frequented my imaginary fascinating woods,
Some moments spent under the sun and the rains,
When actions weren't measured as vane or sane,
I used to be called upon by an imagination game,
At times filling me with joy, other times leaving me lame,
Back then, I was just a child, not chasing a name,
I wasn't onboard one, but I was on a whimsical train.
One such game I played, it involved the roads,
A busy one at that, with vehicles passing in hordes.
I would stand there resting my arms,
On the railing, craning my neck, like a farmer watching a farm,
And I would do nothing but watch passing cars,
And wonder what's faces hid inside, smiles or well hid scars?
Or I'd find myself taking a wild guess,
As to how many were in there, it was my game of finesse.
And whilst caught in that game, I would have easily tamed,
Yet another passage of the time, otherwise mundane.

—————————————Downpourofwords

Footnote: *We all had something in our childhood that we did, that made sense to us, even if it was the most mundane of acts to while away time. Watching passing cars is something I remember clearly as a pass time.*

If a hot iron press wrote?

If I were a hot iron press, what would I do,
Who would be my Master, what would he do?
Or would I have a Mademoiselle unique,
With a wardrobe brimming with glitter and mystique?
Would I be summoned every single day?
Like an elegant tradition that just wouldn't go away,
Or would I be like a mother babysitting her three,
Full of love, with no real sense of 'time for me'?
Would I be found and lost, time and again?
Would I wonder if I make a difference, or burn in vain?
Would there be enough steam in me to inspire some vibes?
For the four walls confine me, but they walked out in style.
I would be watchful I think, I would make my notes,
For then an iron box would have a story, worthy of being told.
——————————————————Downpourofwords

Footnote: *If the things in our daily life had harmless intelligence, to make notes, observations about us, would it in some way enhance our lives? A manifestation of this in today's world is as smartphones. They can measure our heart rate, overall wellbeing, watch our diet and do what else not.*

Opposite of yesterday?

Is yesterday's opposite believed to be tomorrow?
Shouldn't it ethereally be, the NOW?
For yesterday is about what once was,
And today is all about what there is,
And if in contemplation of yesterday,
Our sights get settled on the next day,
I wonder what happens to a day called Today.
Chances are, it will be deftly tucked away,
Just like it's better to see a blur than being totally blind,
There's nothing wrong in keeping the future on our minds,
And in the name of living today, in not planning a future away,
Many a life get entangled, then start looking out for a way.
The secret lies in doing things that make your heart sway,
Not just things done in instantly being carried away.
So why crush today, in tomorrow's hindsight?
Occasionally it's ok to just take it light,
Another yesterday bygone, another tomorrow beckons,
What do we do today, ain't a wonderful question to reckon?

———————————————————————————Downpourofwords

Footnote: *Life in the ethereal sense is more about the yesterday, today and tomorrow, repeatedly at play. It's in these three that we are closest to ourselves and its these three that will always lead the way, to those days where we live the future we imagined for a certain tomorrow.*

Summers & Winters

If I had the gumption, or let's say the absolute Power,
To turn your winter morning's into Summer,
Or your Summer morning's into Winter,
Would that be a magical thing, or rather a bummer?
For all I crave is, to make your heart flutter,
And for that I shall use the truth, not jelly, jam or butter,
And seeing you smile, to me is all that matters,
It doesn't matter if we climb or wade through waters,
I shall keep your feet warm; I know it matters,
You were born in an ice cave, alongside a shower of glitter.
So, tell me now will you, should I use my Power?
To see you blossom amidst alternating Summers & Winters?
Or to leave aside the Power, for it really doesn't matter,
So long as our hearts know, to smile together?
I shall try my best, to keep doing things that matter,
And on days when you feel a tremble, or that nimble stutter,
I shall come running, I got your Summers and Winters.
—————————————————Downpourofwords

Footnote: *Isn't togetherness of two wanting hearts enough to blur the difference between a summer & a winter, a chatter & a banter, a whimsical power & a heartfelt flutter?*

A breed called Fathers

Those innocent stumbles in the initial days,
Patience shown answering the same questions in different ways,
Those words of advice hidden even in games,
Those steely, stern eyes for those mischievous days,
Those silent comforts of always being there,
When the clouds of confusion ruled the air,
Those words of wisdom packed in actions,
Those days spent learning sums, & the fractions,
Those extended hands of comfort for the times in need,
Those positive affirmations for the good deeds,
Those unsaid words that always found a home,
Grew into a mansion now, is dark, wears a look forlorn,
The essence of a good Dad, it lingers in a way that matters,
Here's an ode to all those wonderful Fathers.
————————————————Downpourofwords

Footnote: *If a mother is a guardian angel, a father is a guiding citadel.*
If a mother is a fuzzy bear hug, a father is that necessary tug.

Holding hands

I can feel the fleeting winds in the air,
I can feel something's brewing out there,
There's a calm breeze carrying that scent,
Of a feeling of feeling good in the present.
The wind I feel is one that blows with hope,
It has booby traps set to consume my nope's,
I can sense a white cloud of possibilities, rising above,
Casting a reflection below, that of a green mangrove,
What I also see a dark cloud that's also cold,
Made from petty differences that have most human hearts on hold,
These winds that blow, also carry a blanket along,
To act as a barrier, for them dark clouds above,
A few holes exist, from when humanity went astray,
Acts like holocaust, apartheid tore a big piece away,
The blanket though has two of its ends held,
Held down by two angels, who fly above us, & see the trends,
And they wave the blanket with a smile, that never offends,
As winds of good times into the lives of deserving human beings.
The good times last longer when acts of togetherness fill the air,
For if life's a journey, why walk alone, holding hands seems just fair.

——————————————————————————Downpourofwords

Footnote: *The coldness in your heart shall lead you nowhere, in the end. In kindness & in walking together, there's always something good, around the bend.*

To evolve is a constant

There's not a constant in this world,
For even the warmest of hearts can go cold,
And even the unshakeable at times feel a quiver,
And even in a warm summer, can be felt a shiver.
There's no constant be it people or perceptions alike,
Or for that matter lifeless notions or reputations alike,
What's glorious now can soon be ugly tomorrow
What's livid now can soon be insipid tomorrow.
What's blooming now, can be frozen tomorrow,
What's thriving now can be obsolete tomorrow.
A semblance of constancy it resides though,
In a need to evolve into someone better somehow,
Through the act of dispelling the dark,
And wading on in search of one's truth even if stark,
Juggling between happiness, despair, deceit or hurt,
There's also a constant in keeping on moving forward.
———————————————Downpourofwords

Footnote: *Watch how you feel, every moment, every passing day and what you will realize is that there's no such thing like feeling constant. There's a repetition of a feeling of love, a feeling of belonging, a feeling of longing, a feeling of wanting but there is never an end until the time, that these bones disperse into nothingness, to be one day covered by sand and grime.*

GOT and a Coffee Mug

When all those glaciers that are standing tall,
Will one by one come down crashing, in a monstrous fall,
Would the oceans widen and consume them all?
Or let them barge in into our backyards and walls?
When the sunlight we blissfully cherish, whilst still safe,
Shall soon be dangerous, to burn holes for us to gape,
Would we resign indoors and meekly smile?
For there's internet as a means, to while away the time.
When the air we breathe, becomes available only in traces,
From being poisoned by all kinds of toxic gases,
Would we then gleefully seek refuge in oxygen tanks?
And what shall we do about them hurting backs?
When the time comes, and nature decides to land a nasty tug,
Will we be caught watching GOT, with a coffee mug?

————————————————Downpourofwords

Footnote: *The demise of a glacier can look like a marvelous nature event, until the time that those cascading waters start to rise in an ocean nearby. Or until the point that your favorite beachfront resort is swamped by tides of incoming waves, putting to end your dream vacation spot, watching the sun go down. Read about the mourning for Okjokull glacier or that plaque that read "A Letter to the future". By being blind to the realities of climate change from human inflicted climate change patterns, we are in hindsight bringing down livelihoods of far off families or the chances of repeating a future beach vacation of ours.*

Truth be told

The stings gifted to us in our lives,
Inflicting pains of varying kinds,
Not all of them are meant to stick around,
Not all of those eek out the painful sounds.
A sting from a bee is like a passing fallacy,
A sting from a scorpion, rather a rarity,
A sting from a needle at times, unfortunately a necessity,
In a way, all these external stings are bereft of parity.
It's the stings of a different nature though,
Not driven by nature unlike other stings, truth be told,
Stings inflicted from the creations of a brilliant human mind,
Stings of the heart willfully or unknowingly dealt in life, in kind,
From actions or misplaced emotions in our day to day lives,
Hurting everyone from kids to adults to a loving wife,
The pain from external stings will one day be long gone,
Whilst the stings of the heart, they cling, and hang around.
————————————————Downpourofwords

Footnote: *Pain like the air we breathe, is omnipresent n life. Some face it many a times while some face it by and far but in monstrous proportions. When we know that pain in life is inevitable, it's in how to deal with it that assumes prominence. Yet, as we walk through life, there are people whom we see, who have mastered the act of inflicting pain for an unexplained form of hidden pleasure, in the form of hurtful words, disrespect, a disregard driven by selfishness, inducing stress in the lives of another through abuse of power. Each of us, in some way have caused pain to someone, intentional or not. Imagine each of the 4 billion plus people on planet Earth taking a pledge to avoid one form of pain big or small, in our lifetime. That's many a billion less aching hearts. Kindness & compassion are our ways out of the pain.*

Temporary banter

On days when you feel literally lost,
With a feeling of being stuck in the same spot,
As your mind wanders, in between silent thoughts,
And the eerie silence infuses them uncomfortable knots,
Into your senses, making it a battle hard to cope,
With that empty feeling, accompanied by a lack of hope,
All is need, to ask yourself is what have I done?
And what is it that I plan on getting done,
And what would it feel like when I am really done,
Battling these worries, with my acts, to imagine myself having won.
If the vision you see feels alright, take a breath, in silence,
A deep one at that, and in that silent moment,
For in seeing yourself free of them worries, is in a way,
Your answer to how you shall carve out your own way.
Realize as well, that you are not alone, as many others,
Also keep feeling this ruffling of their inner feathers.
In the end, it's not such empty moments that really matter,
It's how you deal wisely with that temporary banter.

—————————————————Downpourofwords

Footnote: *There is strength in unity, and it's an omnipresent truth. This strength can be drawn upon even in the act of knowing that we are not alone, in facing the crisis we face today. That there are a million others juggling the same worries, at this very moment. The thought however is not enough to carve out a way, and that's when the might in imagining oneself, bereft of those worries comes into play. Don't let it go waste. Invest away.*

Trending Virus

Trends are what trend in today's world,
From how to make coffee to warding off that nightly cold,
From the shoes we wear to the charade of stairs,
Life seems to be filled with never ending shades.
From the memes we watch to how the way we talk,
From choices to wear to spending time in the neighborly park.
From viral videos to neatly morphed viral photographs,
The viral virus pervasively keeps calling them shots,
From where to travel, to taking a flawless selfie guide,
From where to pose, to posing elegantly with vibes,
Where vacations seem more a way to flaunt with pride,
Measured by moments shared on social media, with much else to hide,
Where bucket lists as well seem to be virally picked,
With way too many options for the mind to be incessantly tricked.
What goes viral seems to catch on like wildfire,
With everyone else making it their newfound desire,
Makes me wonder what it is that's really aspired,
In acting upon trends, not much from being inspired.
——————————————————Downpourofwords

Footnote: *Mildly put, it's from a want to do something and be well known, a want for self-validation that drives the need to act like others. Harshly, & more truthfully put, its known as the herd mentality. Our acts need not be a silent usher into this herd mentality. The hold their essence if they are driven from our core, not from a frivolous necessity.*

Those silent talks

The silence that I notice in your eyes,
Seems unnerving to start with, other times like a vice,
I wonder what it intends to convey though,
I see a look of belonging, yet also a vindicating look, so low,
What I also notice is a glare – from being heartbroken,
And trust me, this feeling in me doesn't erupt that very often.
It's faint though and I yet I see it leaving me confused,
Is it hatred for what you did, or my mind acting bemused?
In that moment of a mere contemplation,
I elope with your silence and make my own reflections,
The inner me though - blames you innocently,
For not having looked deeper, a little more firmly,
And I see myself looking within me, for my frailties,
With a look of acceptance of our Love, as a necessity,
And then I hope to latch on, to that inexplicable affinity,
That we both crave, amidst all our sanity, and insanities.
The next time though I shall try to make a move,
Until then here's sending you an image of the sky so blue.
————————————————Downpourofwords

Footnote: *Arguments are not there to create a divide, all the time. If there is a reflection at both ends as to the reasons for an argument & acceptance of what needs to change, what can be better, Love shall still prevail, and it does. In magical ways.*

A Playlist our own

Sing me that unpopular song will you,
The one that only me and you can listen through,
For its so stark and quintessentially unique,
Often dismissed as just another high-flying cliché,
For us though, the song makes for an ocean of absolute sense,
Dispelling any sense of the worldly false pretense.
The words from the song, laid out as pearls,
Touch upon moments we felt, cause those flutters,
We stumbled upon that song merely by chance,
I thank the stars, for it upholds our blissful trance,
A trance that you and I feel, whenever the song plays,
A feeling out of this world, in more than many ways.
One song though cannot define our hearts sway,
And I love my music, my fingers don't hurt from hitting play,
Come along now, I've my playlist set,
Let's recollect those moments, since the time we first met.

——————————————Downpourofwords

Footnote: *What are those unique songs in your playlist that make you relive memories with someone close, someone special, someone you Love? Is there a hidden playlist known to only the two of you?*

Sports and Life

What is it about watching sports?
That creates a cauldron made of hordes,
Of hopeful people wanting to enthusiastically watch,
Watch a possibility meeting its prized catch,
That of opportunity in a game to win or to lose,
To then relate it to our own battles, like a muse.
I have an inkling that sports are also watched,
In that little time of being lost in a game, imagination caught,
To be able to derive some inspiration of sorts,
To be able to fight harder in life, even if in parts.
And in those moments spent following the tactics,
Making mental notes on strategies and them possibilities,
There's a subconscious inference that goes on inside,
Relating to one's own battle, albeit from a different side,
And unlike life where battles seem often long drawn,
A game offers an ending conveniently, even if short and small.
————————————Downpourofwords

Footnote: *I have often found myself caught in awe of the sea of fans that make it their life to support their favorite teams & have at some point felt drawn myself into that feeling. If we probe deeper, one of the reasons we watch sports is to derive inspiration from the victors or from seeing a defeat turn over into a victory later.*

Readers Digest

On a memory train that I recently took,
There was this presence of a reading nook,
Alongside some blurry images of my childhood,
It was something about reading a book.
I remember that place on the second floor,
Of an elderly neighbor who was a college Professor,
His thought brings about an image of a manly voice,
That resonated with words he plucked, as his choice,
There was a stack full of books out there,
One section though, always caught my glare,
A pile of Reader's Digest stacked up real neat,
Open for me to borrow, for my thirsty reading beak,
The Professor's long gone but to the gesture of his,
I stand today, to bow & blow a gratitude filled kiss,
For what he loaned to me back then was a freedom,
To dive in into words, making my own sense, even if random.
————————————————————Downpourofwords

Footnote: *This poem is inspired by a memory of a relative, a college Professor named D.B.Patil who is no more, yet his essence lives in me through his gesture. A gesture of allowing me to lend those Reader's Digests for whenever I wanted, if I returned them in the state that I received them in. Thank you, Sir. RIP.*

Watch Out

You think you got me all figured out,
And your moves against me, deftly worked out,
If you think you have me all measured up,
I grin at that and raise my collar higher on up.
For you don't have any inkling that I have layered up,
Structured levels of belief, that I often I conjure up,
For when needed, all I do is pull a string,
And I sense a shower of a comforting, positive inkling,
Lifting me up and I feel my nerves relaxing,
Weird though even in situations quite unnerving.
The mountains you think you keep dishing out,
I got workman like moles to grind them to the ground,
All I am saying here is for you to watch out,
For you shall regret the day that my tank of patience dries out.
——————————————————————————————Downpourofwords

Footnote: *In a room full of people I will always be amongst the top 10% in terms of my mild manners. Yet, when provoked the wrong way, for quite some time, I have an ocean of strength that I could summon to leave you gasping for breath, if I decided to take it that far. Watch out.*

Spoken words

More than seven billion people on planet Earth,
A zillion words at least, every day uttered,
I think about that and stand in admiration,
What a blissful gift, is that of communication.
I take a pause and drool at that thought,
Empathy fills my heart for being's that can't,
Empathy from not being able to bring to life those feelings,
Felt by even the mute humans & all the other species,
Which in a game of evolution, got left behind;
Yet upholding the best of life's lessons, as their lives unwind.
A channel between the heart and the mouth,
Is the gift of speaking, where the words come out,
I wonder what percentile of the Zillion words spoken daily,
Do get spoken from the heart, truthfully.
—————————————————Downpourofwords

Footnote: *Imagine a day of your life without being able to speak. How does that feel? It would then dawn upon us as to the immense gratitude in the act of being able to communicate. Yet we all know that most words that get spoken are not true. Can we try and increase the percentile? It's in the red, from where I see, but to the other side, there is always that green.*

Where virtues once resided

There's a certain way of having fun,
Inside our minds, through observation,
For human behavior when scanned under the sun,
At times, is funnier than any known imagination.
Life is short yet long enough to show,
Many a seasons' where the time just flows,
And more than the seasons that change,
You shall often notice something quite strange,
Dispelling the laws of physics, as well as entities,
In acts where people keep changing their identities,
Not by name but somewhere deep inside,
Where once a firm nest of virtues resided.
And to see that strength behind the words full of lies,
Spoken to your face boldly, as truth whimpers & cries,
When both sides know where their priorities lie,
One headed to a place of calm, the other on a ghastly ride.
If you see close enough and start to compare,
Compare them then and now, you'll start to enjoy this game.
—————————————————————Downpourofwords

Footnote: *This poem is a dedication to all those people who master
the act of concealing their empty souls, and do so very well under neatly
placed words, knowing very well they are wrong, yet riding along, on
ropes of authority or power which they grabbed once feverishly. Just know
that we know; that you know, what waters you wade, and how low.*

If I woke up as a "----"

What if I wake up one fine day?
To see the mirror in shock, and scream away,
From waking up having a beak on my face,
And feathers that I could nonchalantly flaunt in grace,
To try and speak, and hear a chirp but the words won't come out,
Yet retain my human intellect, to stand apart in a chirpy crowd,
Would I fly to that seemingly haunting windowsill?
Or fly further to look in wonder again at those hills,
And from a mountain, would I take that blind leap of faith,
Or shiver in my claws, to ponder giving up, to wait,
Even if I did it right and flew into the air alright,
My chirps even if melodious, would my claws let me write?
For being away from the bliss in writing, in itself is a fright,
Larger than wanting to a bird, just to soar into the skies.
A life without writing my thoughts, doesn't seem alright,
Even if I could be a beautiful bird in those skies.

———————————————Downpourofwords

Footnote: *To wish to be something else, someone else is a though that crosses our minds many a times. At what cost, is something to be dwelled into, in hindsight.*

Something you can hold

Long ago once upon a time,
Life was simple, breathing was just fine,
But then a wave started, it emanated out of inventing,
It grew into an insatiable, hunger to go on reinventing,
A few Eureka's here, a few Eureka's there,
In the beginning, it all seemed just fair,
An invention for comfort, an invention for strength,
An invention for longevity, another one for mindfulness,
And before we knew, we had an inventory so massive,
Life is now spent choosing, what else to have, being submissive.
We raged a dream drunk war and got so far,
At times skidding on our backs, with our mouth ajar,
In admiration most times from what we found out,
And we kept skidding far and further on out.
I wonder if we ran too fast too far,
Even went light years away, came back from touching a star,
In all this while, a lot has changed,
From swiping flies to swiping a living person's face,
From admiring hearts to being lured by external mettle,
Our backs hurts from all the skidding our desires won't be embezzled,
And I read an article about levitation, as a means of transport,
We shall skid faster now, hang on to something you can hold.

——————————————————Downpourofwords

Footnote: *Has the humankind gone too far in exploring the adventure in invention, not limiting it to things that matter, and let Eureka's run amok in all aspects, to be scattered? And with the inventions of all kinds, do we have more time spent choosing than in time spent living?*

Poor Little Johnny

The door to their living room was locked,
There was a loud noise as someone knocked!
There were six of them inside yet not a sound-
-Made its way from the omnipresent silence around,
The knocks grew louder, so did their restlessness that swelled,
Breathing heavy, reluctantly shoving the silence aside,
From fear, within the shivering family inside,
Praying those fearful knocks would somehow, subside,
And to add to the melee, the doorbell then rang,
Soon turning into a rhythm of chimes, followed by violent bangs,
Little Johnny wet his pants, he couldn't hold on,
Not knowing what danger is, but rather reacting along,
His much awaited, well planned family TV night,
Why did it have to turn into a night full of frights?
The family played a prank on the little kid,
By simulating those sounds, from a corner well hid,
—————————————————————Downpourofwords

Footnote: *The harmless pranks that are well played out, often end up bringing a much-awaited laughter, and togetherness there on out.*

The unfinished poem

I always wanted to write a poem,
To then crown it as an 'unfinished Poem'
With words that made it solemn and soothing,
Sprinkling some glitter of playful rhyming,
And invoke a feeling about a random something,
Yet not knowing what it is, that's tinkling,
For when there's no intent, but just a feeling,
There's a sense of hidden pleasure in plainly knowing,
That the senses do linger, without a hint of quiver,
And in that silent moment some place far, not near,
Inside a heart, it leaves a fleeting trace,
Of an unnamed moment, laden with grace,
That moment adds a meaning to my writing,
A poem that I once wrote without titling,
For in the mystery of that hidden feeling,
Lies the victory of this weird-some writing.
———————————————————Downpourofwords

Footnote: *At times, words have that power to take us on a ride where there is no set destination in mind yet the journey spent dispelling in different types of words and the way they were laid down, that in itself is worth the while.*

The comeback icon

On a gruesome night out in the cold,
A man once straddled on, acting bold,
Concealing the shiver in his spine, rather old,
In a torn jean, and wearing a neat jacket in gold,
Had words '**Once a Star**' smudged and smeared,
In bright red resembling the brightest red,
He hummed a tune in a voice that had turned hoarse,
Of a man who had once found his calling in his throat,
A life where he had found a new beginning,
Through the blissful act of heart-felt singing,
A dash of arrogance then, hadn't gone well with the crowd,
They left no stone unturned, blatantly crowned him lost,
He tried to explain himself, but his time had run out,
The verdict had been made; he had been called out.
The man though picked up his words and sounds,
And went on living life the way he knew, in making songs,
Until one day, one of his songs climbed along,
Till it topped the charts, and stood bold and strong,
And guess what, the same crowd hopped back on,
Filled up the palladiums, named him a comeback icon,
And he smiled in his mind, knowing all along,
He never went anywhere; he was with his songs.

—————————————Downpourofwords

Footnote: *Faintly inspired by Eminem's comeback attempts so far and also applicable to many an artist who fall out of public favor to then come back stronger than before. The only thing that makes it happen is being in connect with what got them there in the first place.*

An Ode to Art

There's a sense of belonging in being part,
Of a quintessential act of creating Art,
For it's a pure blessing to act from the heart,
Throwing caution into the winds, far on out.
It's those moments of being consumed,
By a presence of one's own world, rather unused,
Where being free in thought, is a lovely symphony,
Where dreams go on a date with creativity.
And at times when on that romantic date,
A few thoughts get heartfully exchanged,
Between an Artist's mind and an invisible realm,
Filled with friendly siblings named as distant dreams.
They pass on a candle to the ones who fight,
If what they create soulfully, feels blissfully right.

—————————————————Downpourofwords

Footnote: *When an artist dispels in her/his art and connects with an imaginary realm to create art, it is a true amalgamation of human imagination & the process of giving life to something magical.*

Change the station

If all the frailties of the human mind,
Were to be tied up in a cohesive bind,
And tossed into an abysmal black hole,
I wonder what would happen of the world,
For frailties do sing a mesmerizing song,
With a feeble presence, yet humming along,
Into our conscience, with a mournful gong,
Scuttling the life out of our hopeful songs,
Only time shall tell if such an abyss would hold,
Amidst loathing and gnawing by frailties that are seldom not bold,
For if they (people & thyself) can weaken a hopeful soul,
The human mind to them, none less than a rabbit in a hole.
The next time you hear that mournful gong,
Change the station and sing a song, one your own.
—————————————Downpourofwords

Footnote: *It is in the nature of a human mind to worry. Our experiences circumstances & often times our thoughts are bound to be around worries. It's an art to keep worrying yet be actionable in trying to get those worries away.*

That unique place

Sometimes I find myself in a unique place,
A flash of that image though, seen in my present,
Through an event, or some feeble incident,
Or at times as a beautiful coincidence,
I see myself standing ahead of where-
-I was once, carrying a look of despair,
Despair from the choices I had nonchalantly made,
When all I needed was one single path to tread,
And there I was, caught up in a hypnotic swirl,
Tossed and turned into a twisted telltale,
But there's something about that unique place,
I am lagging still, but I have worked up my pace,
For I see myself falling short in this world, but way ahead,
Of where I once was, lonely, desolate looking and stranded.
————————————Downpourofwords

Footnote: *At times it pays to look at where we stand today &*
to reflect on whether we are in a better place than before.

Connecting the Dots

Even in the unlikeliest of places,
We can paint our own colorful spaces,
If we learn the act of bracing ourselves,
Even in bits and pieces, and learn to take them chances,
To keep away the laundry list of action items,
Hurled by life at us, at regular intervals,
To revel in a few moments of blissful existence,
To rekindle the sense of life, one of an awakened conscience,
Through a few moments spent in nothing else but silence,
Of nothing but nimble thoughts and their fleeting essence.
The laundry list would have stayed on anyway,
But why let a moment of tranquil slip away?
For in this simple act where we learn to disconnect,
Do a few missing dots of life, solemnly connect;.
———————————————————————————————————————Downpourofwords

Footnote: *Mindfulness is a conscious act of disconnecting from the mundane and reveling in thoughts no matter what, consciously. Every now and then, we should disconnect from a thought evoked by seeing something on the phone, on the television or something about what someone said, did and purely dispel in carefree thoughts whatever they maybe, for a while. To feel their presence, the essence, to realize that our minds can think deeply & not always be directed, if we allow it to feel that state.*

The Batman Kite

An old man who was declared as senile,
By his family, even the young one's juvenile,
Who the old man had selflessly taught to fly,
In their backyard that is, after umpteen tries,
To fly high into a beautiful blue sky,
Through something that he'd made, a Batman kite.
His fault though, was that he could see their flaws,
He had his opinion on life, knew the unwritten laws,
And at times when he caught hold of their lies,
They found themselves swatted, like a lethargic fly.
But to the learned ones who read some books on life,
His every word and act seemed like pinching acts, senile,
What he thought he was, came crashing down,
Like a white mansion he built from scratch, hammered down,
As the rubble and the dust cleared, he clearly saw,
The royalty was only in his mind, he a lowly Grandpa,
For his wisdom was looked upon as out of line,
To the generation riding on codes, a billion lines,
He seeks his peace now, in an isolated asylum,
He still pens down his thoughts, as words of wisdom.
————————————————Downpourofwords

Footnote: *As someone who has had to live most of his life without
the blissful presence of parents, I always wonder what makes
all those old age homes swell in numbers, year after year?*

Horizons with no skies

Give me all your flaws, give it to me raw,
Give me all your reasons, give it to me now,
Give me your notions, hand them on a saw,
Give me all your fears, I'll make them thaw,
Give me everything you got, and we won't have to look back,
Give in with your heart, I will delete that word 'lack'.
Give in with your smiles, for me to toss in my collections bag,
Give in, not with attitude, and make me like your swag,
Give in with your confusions, for I like untying knots,
Give in with your feelings, I shall dispel in your thoughts.
Give in with your troubles, I'll bludgeon them with my tries,
Give in with your soul, for only then can we fly,
Fly we shall one day, into a horizon with no skies,
Where spreading arms is like staying still yet feeling the wind for miles.
——————————————————Downpourofwords

Footnote: *When you accept someone, you accept them for who they are. And it's often times a mix of good, not so good, their quirks, their tantrums, their crystal-clear flaws, their everything that includes even the little gestures that make them, them.*

A Pyramid Poem

I
Am one
With words plenty
I
Am one
With wings sturdy
I
Am one
Step below Sanity
I
Am one
Rung above Vanity.

Footnote: *Every stanza is made of three lines and six words each. The character count increases by one with every word from one character to six.*

Questions

If you are a fiction of my imagination,
Why do I sense this anticipation?
If you are the action in my emotions,
Why do I sense these convulsions?
If you are the rationale in my decisions,
Why do I sense these confusions?
If you are the air that I breathe,
Why do I sense this restless breeze?
If you are the wind beneath my wings,
Why do I spin amidst spiraling winds?
If you are a faction of my portion,
Why do I sense this separation?
If you are a part of my own being?
Is there any sense then, in not belonging?
————————————————Downpourofwords

Footnote: *Isn't is also purely human to feel torn between thoughts, feelings, emotions and questions that sometimes seem to have no rationale?*

Like a Dream

Treat a woman like you treat a dream,
Nurture her and show her what she means,
Cherish her like you cherish your dream,
Take her to places you have never seen.
Treat a woman like you passionately chase making a name,
Anticipate her feelings, don't be standing, looking lame,
Keep your eyes wrapped onto her, like a satin string,
Cheering her on and her every little feeling.
Treat a woman like you treat a baby,
Caring as hell, harmlessly overprotective, a maybe.
Notice her innocence and learn some ignorance,
Cajole her, whilst being her charming prince,
Treat her well but as a man, never ever forget,
How to be a man of vision, who breaks a sweat.
————————————————Downpourofwords

Footnote: *There are certain things that make women, women. One of them is seeking care, love, attention and acceptance. If arrogance or being logically inclined is an acceptable trait for men, these are too, for women. Moderation though in expectations, matters on both sides.*

Love undead?

I asked you a question many times,
What is it that moves you inside?
All you did was to fake it and hide,
While you looked to take me on a ride,
Now when my storms are finally quiet,
And when I have moved on away, found my stride,
There you are again, calling on my help,
Like I am just a wayward floating oceanic kelp,
That you can hang on to for a little while,
Until you have found another have, something worthwhile,
To then wave me a goodbye with a smile,
And expecting me to turn back and smile.
I told you my mind was right,
When you were lost in a measly fight,
About something so trivial, so light,
The rage I feel inside, still gives me a fright.
I will still stand by your other side,
But hey, I think my Love for you that lived once, has died.
—————————————————Downpourofwords

Footnote: *It is but natural to come face to face with hurt, in Love, in relationships, in bonds that we make in life. Not everything that gets broken can be fixed, not every feeling of acceptance can be mixed. Like a flower vase made of glass can be tried to be put together but it can never be the same.*

A bottle I tossed

I tossed my feelings into a bottle,
Corked it tight, then heard it rattle,
A quirky sound it made, by no means nimble,
Squeaked hard wanting out, to innocently snuggle,
These were feelings evoked by a kind of separation,
Of someone who once, was a loved one.
I caught it with slippery fingers that bled,
Cut by the cork that miraculously until then, had firmly held,
My slippery fingers held onto it rather well,
Got all her feelings in, and I saw them swell,
I stood by the sea, drenched in a moment of reflection,
Before dispelling the quivering bottle, into the ocean,
The next morning at work, on my table,
I sat grinning, staring at the same damn bottle.

—————————————————Downpourofwords

Footnote: *At times, the mind wants to throw someone's thoughts out into the open sea, but failure is not only in the things we do, it can be in the things we think as well.*

Soldiers and Fate

Spare a thought for those rangers,
Who go in on a date with a stranger,
Every so often, without much of a banter,
As if on a break, or heading home for supper,
But the love affair with that stranger,
Is one which makes most people's insides shudder,
For when the date is with a real monster,
Raising an ugly hood, a lover named Danger,
Uncertainty, it exists just like in a usual date,
But the stakes are higher, reaching as far as fate.
Being a soldier is living life on a blank slate,
There's a lot more to love, much less to hate,
Where days are measured not in knowing its cold or warm,
But spent flirting with danger, in time believing it to be a norm,
A job needing you to rethink about your own impending fate,
Deserves a kneeling Salute - Here you go, Mates.
—————————————————Downpourofwords

Footnote: *How difficult is it to imagine oneself as a Soldier, a Cop or someone in Security, when there is uncertainty, about life itself? What does it take to put your life on the line not once but at every incident, if the job description calls for it? Often, I see news about corrupt police, corrupt law enforcement officials as a big deal. It is something to deal with for sure. But there's corruption in every other job that's done, without a fear of losing one's life. It's painful to see that a service that deserved more respect is pulled down quite often by incidents by and far. Respect the ones in service.*

Sculptures in my mind

I often wonder if I'm genetically hardwired,
With neatly labeled blue sculptures, in my mind,
For certain decisions that I often make,
Seem to be reading labels, from someplace else,
Makes me wonder what those labels read,
And a shiver runs down my spine, causing me dread.
What if those referential sculptures are wrong?
Would I be traveling too far, to then be long gone?
That's when I open my eyes to a realm of vibrant color,
And I see all hues looking at me in wonder,
The sculptures not in blue are from other people,
And I can see that they too have them labels.
In not being fully blinded by one's own blues,
To be open to vibrant colors from others, is in accepting perceptions new,
Is life long or short? It shall remain an unsolved mystery,
Whilst here. learning from other's vibes, isn't that a necessity.

———————————————————Downpourofwords

Footnote: *We all have our beliefs around how we want to do things, how we intend for things to pan out and it's all but natural. But to be blind to learning from others is a fallacy best when avoided. To fail and learn is a good thing. But to fail at everything and learning everything on one's own, would need a few lifetimes. It is good to learn from other's experiences, advice, and vibes. And when you learn from others directly or indirectly, please drop in a thank you note. It takes effort for someone to inspire acts of good. And no one has ever lost anything by acknowledging the good.*

The unsung hordes

Is there ever a semblance of a thought?
About all the battles that were fought,
Into which men and women walked in hordes,
Even if the thought of fighting didn't strike a chord,
Deep inside the hearts, where their beliefs lived,
But fate had other plans, intentions higher were peeved,
And a matter of life or death had been sealed,
In an envelope stamped by a man driven by power and needs,
A need more for oneself, than for ones in need,
At times under a guise of crushing ugly hoods of misdeeds,
Or other times, driven by good for the human creed,
For in drastic times, peace is through nipping that violent seed,
Those lives are long gone, served, assuming a need,
Those losses justified or not, how many care to read?
While all we are busy doing, browsing through one's glittery feed,
To name a day, celebrate it and move on, conscience again emptied,
Makes me wonder, not all battles are of the right kind,
Some fought for answers to find, others from being caught in a bind.
————————————Downpourofwords

Footnote: *The soldiers who put their lives at stake living by
the country's decisions, they need a little more appreciation
than being remembered on celebrated days only.*

Adversities

Random musings, intent filled cravings,
Tandem feelings, hardened ailing's,
Platonic bonding's, frivolous dating,
Enticing frailties, unforgiving penalties,
Connected thoughts, Pointless conversations,
Visionary visions, momentary distractions,
Blissful relations, a broken heart's palpitations,
Concise directions, wayward intentions,
Enlightened empathy, self-bred apathy,
Heightened sanctity, unnerving tenacity,
Virtuous qualities, demonic frailties,
Abundant journeys, half lived fallacies,
Awkwardly soulful, comfortably forgetful,
Magnificently truthful, connivingly deceitful,
A happy state of mind, cursing fate, being spiteful,
Carpe diem way, waiting to live life another day.
————————————Downpourofwords

Footnote: *Life oftentimes is a mishmash of varied emotions that we all feel and to be born and human and have the ability to rationale comes with the ability to feel. It is impossible to avoid the barrage of feelings good or bad, but it is possible to channel them, work with them and find the right ways to wade through the difficult ones, to try and find a balance. Fitness consciousness, mindfulness, meditation of some sort, reading books and a few ways I have found some sort of a balance, while I keep stumbling ever so often, with a smile.*

A Pedestal Some Place

Place me on a pedestal some place,
From where I could see through every face,
And be able to look within, for a trace,
That belies words coming out of those lips, most often with grace.
For if most words spoken had a truth,
Wouldn't life be more blissful, plainly put?
Would the whims and fantasies of the human mind;
Then try and dispel another *'Can't'*, to enrich the humankind?
For once, with acts carrying them selfish bones, none,
Or them treacherous acts, with hideous victories won,
As it stands now, without such a pedestal on which to heave,
It's hard to know what to believe, what not to believe.
If the mind and heart from everyone around got aligned,
And words spoken were true, bereft of any lies,
I wonder where we would be today, as Humankind,
A million nautical miles ahead I suppose, at least in my mind.

—————————————————Downpourofwords

Footnote: *One of the most powerful gifts of humanity is in straddling along, together. Yet, there are differences even in the simplest of decisions, in acceptance, in acts filled with hollow promises which make people fake the words they speak so boldly. If the petty differences could for once be trashed, I believe humanity would have father to go, faster.*

An invention so meaningful

Of all the inventions of glorious humankind,
One tamely lurks, yet nonchalantly shines,
It's not a technology as such, of any kind,
Just another masterstroke, from a thoughtful mind.
The invention of a mirror, so to speak,
Is a glorious one, hides many answers we seek,
For a simple act of looking in the mirror, at oneself,
Isn't it an act of self-reflection, if nothing else?
But more often than not, in this thing called life,
A look in the mirror is without a hindsight,
For even if the truth stares back in all its might,
There's an ignorance that's learned, it eases the ride.
Don't we all at times, look back into the mirror,
Looking for an omnipresent, yet invisible answer?
And without thanking the inventor, don't we all wonder,
If this is the best I can be, or there's more thunder?
And to find oneself asking *"why me, why was I sent this way, as this?"*
What is my purpose, what have I missed?
———————————————Downpourofwords

Footnote: *A life without purpose is a never-ending stream
of thoughts starting with "I Suppose". And what better than
a mirror to dwell into those questions that matter?*

Animals

As I wonder sometimes, in my free time,
A tumultuous thought, it crosses my weird some mind,
Comes along uninvited, knowing it would be just fine,
For thoughts are forever welcome, in a Writer's mind.
Did something change it wonders, at some point in time,
Or was humanity always this social since Adam and Eve's time?
Was there a fear of the unknown long ago, so deep?
For we humans then as well, had distances to keep,
Or were we born with them social genes inside,
That made waking and sleeping together a possible ride?
If we weren't bestowed to get along, then what did ensue?
Was it loneliness, a wish, or a dream-too good to be true?
That made us build our homes next to one another,
To then call it a Society, to try and prosper together?
If we were like that, where did we falter along,
Now letting hatred, intolerance, and violence spread their deadly pangs?
In the act of humans treating humans, as animals,
Would it be fair to rename all life then, as Animals?
——————————————————Downpourofwords

Footnote: *If there was a video recording of life, as it evolved over the ages, the act of being social as a species would be a fascinating story to watch. History has examples of socialism turn into animosity and into enmity, to leave behind scars that we still try to shove, under the blankets of time. The world luckily is in better times today and most battles are fought in the mind, but if we look at it as a society, there are still sections of people we ignore, who deserve more.*

A Demon who cares

If a sunset so befalls on Mother Earth,
For one final time, for what it's worth,
Would it be slow, like a chain of sequential events?
Or rather an abrupt end to everything that's existent?
Would each catastrophe point to the demon that beckons?
A demon not that cold hearted, for he gives us indications,
Before he would finally engulf us in his rage,
For in all fairness, he had howled out loud, to turn the page.
If things one day, did come to a spiteful end,
Would we still be caught up chasing them trends?
For it could all be put to an end, with one swift, silken strike,
An act of penance, to life for having spiked too high,
Where the gift called awareness went for an intoxicated swim,
Into them high seas, to be there, and to never be seen.
A heavenly abode is Mother Earth, to be experienced with pride,
And the detours were built long ago, knowing we could ride,
Why wait to see those signs, count on a demon being kind?
When all it takes is taking one baby step at a time,
The time was never righter, to set it back alright,
For even the demon known to cause an end, wants us to survive.

——————————————————————Downpourofwords

Footnote: *Baby steps here refers to paper/cloth grocery bags,
donating to plant a tree, recycling paper and the like.*

Riddles of Life

If the mind is a mysterious riddle,
Why then, is there a thoughtful huddle?
If life is an illustrious unending battle,
Why then, are dreams so enticing & beautiful?
If victories are measured by the bruises taken,
Why then, do miracles seem to occur at random?
If the journey of life is measured in the miles gone,
Why then, do certain ambiences feel like home?
If the heart is a potpourri of inexplicable emotions,
Why then, is there power of intellect in us humans?
If most feelings are full of misguided intentions,
Why then, are there still flourishing relations?
If life's a game of cat and mouse unending,
Why then, does the demon of death stare, beckoning?
—————————————————Downpourofwords

Footnote: *Life is a potpourri of conflicting events, things, feelings
and situations. What comes out of it is mystically profound
at times whilst heartbreakingly mediocre other times. It is in
what we make out of every situation, that really counts.*

Cryptic Sync

Nobody knows you the way I do,
This confidence in me is pure and true,
And I know that the essence of me,
That you feel deep inside, when you breathe,
That sigh of relief, the peaceful moment you feel,
From a sense of belonging, not from a need,
Is what makes you, you - someone very sweet,
And in knowing you this way, I feel a new kind of free.

I didn't plan on planting those seeds,
Love seeks flowers, doesn't step on weeds,
I have known you through your layers,
Unraveled you at times, with an animalistic fervor,
At times being spellbound, for you stole my thunder,
From what lay beneath those layers, deep down under,
And when two hearts decide to beat, in a cryptic sync,
Is when feelings attain a new meaning, unique,
And this feeling isn't sold in factories of lust and greed,
A cryptic sync open to decoding only by ones in Love indeed.
——————————————————————Downpourofwords

Footnote: *The blissful feeling of Love is oftentimes a difficult topic to write on. It can be expressed but never defined. Love is a limitless feeling that can be experienced to be believed.*

Lost in New York

On a winter night some place in New York,
Wandered a lonely man ubiquitously lost,
For everywhere he looked, he saw them squares,
Looking down upon him, with haunting glares,
Those sliver rocks so pristine and sprinkling light,
Seemed to mesmerize his joyful eyes,
Joyous from the beauty, but fearful at heart,
Of stepping into an alien world, a world that looked apart.

In the abode to which he, by birth belonged,
Life was divine, blissful, peaceful and people smiled a lot,
But neither people not the monuments were square,
Their only sparkling possession at most, was a glistening spear,
And as he missed his home, he felt an irksome fear,
What if he could never get home, oh dear!
What he saw here was comfort, but a path unclear,
Whilst back home, all he had was a tree and his river,
And his family of three, **Nadaiva**, **Ulaiva** and **Godiva**.
He had set sail to touch a Sealion, and seek a blessing,
Had lost his sail, to then be lost in New York City.

———————————————-Downpourofwords

Footnote: *What if a human who calls nature as his abode is left in the middle of New York City? What would his thoughts be?*

A cup of tea please?

Make me a cup of tea, will you?
I love the set of motions, you go through,
In making that hot cup of tea, ever so gently,
Is a sight that touches my heart, ever so deftly,
I am an admirer of facts, for they are known to be true,
And science does nail them facts, even seals a glue.
One such fact, is that water shall always boil,
At a certain pace, bound by fire beneath, and time,
Which is exactly what I soulfully seek,
Moments of watching you, beautiful and sleek,
Engaged in a simplistic routine, with that lovely smile,
On what I shall say, after sipping your chai.
The most mesmerizing of all though, is that smile,
That you give me when I make a cup of Chai,
And to hand it to you like a Princess on an elegant high,
Is what I find my little moment of bliss beneath my sky,
And so, I decided to keep serving you a lifetime of Chai's,
To keep finding my comforts under your eye lashes & your smiles.

—————————————————Downpourofwords

Footnote: *At times, it's not the bigger acts filled with grandeur that define Love. It is the little gestures done ever so often that redefine the essence of Love.*

A Parallel World

Can a parallel world be tried out some place?
A World bereft of the monetary concept,
Where societal levels drawn purely on good,
With not much hanging on collecting the moolah or gold,
For then, there won't be any of those debts to be paid,
In a society with virtues act as foundations, well laid,
And if righteous actions of people, acts of spreading some smiles,
Become a scale on which, measured are people's lives,
Where wisdom and kindness define the quality of life,
Not one's ability to wade through, flashing knives.
Where an abundant life is based on how worthwhile,
A person is as oneself and towards other life,
Where there's always a hand for the ones that are willing,
To dispel in the art takes, in making it worthwhile,
The art of being kind, and the art of sharing & giving,
The art of being helpful, and the art of forgetting & forgiving,
If such acts get lauded as positives that make a society great,
And are scored as such, on an equally plain slate.
And the people who act like crabs, who try to make a steal,
Are left lurking in lower societal ranks, to fight or to heal,
Where the only way up the ranks is through being good,
With one's virtues defining shelter, prosperity and food.

—————————————Downpourofwords

Footnote: *If our society was taken up to a drawing board, to start to redefine the ways to success & prosperity, and base it on virtues, acts of kindness, ability to create in one's area of interest, I wonder what the world would look and feel like? I see a every portrait of people shining with more smiles.*

To evolve is a constant

There's not a certain constant in this world,
For everything can change in ways unheard, untold,
Be it the people or the perceptions alike,
Be it the notions or the repercussions alike,
What's glorious now can quickly be ugly tomorrow,
What's livid now can soon be insipid tomorrow,
What's blooming now, can be frozen tomorrow,
What's thriving now, can be forgotten tomorrow,
A semblance of a constant it resides though,
In the need to evolve all the way through,
As a change inside, and on the outside,
Where fear, possibilities, and even demons reside,
And only through the act of dispelling in one's dark,
Can there be a consistency be found, to act as a spark,
With happiness, despair, deceit or hurt,
Being the experiences in life to evolve, word.
———————————————————————————Downpourofwords

Footnote: *To be constant in life, is a death of sorts. To not feel change constantly in life, is a wayward wish of sorts. And it's in between these two, life gets lived in parts.*

A Unicorn Cut loose

Somewhere in one corner of the world,
A species hibernates in inhumane cold,
We humans even coined up a word,
Called it inhumane, for we as a species, are brazenly bold,
Bold from the intellect bestowed upon us all,
By nature, so we could wish for, and have it all.
Somewhere in another remote place elsewhere,
A species waits all day, to play hunger games,
To venture out in dark, only to be safe,
And to find it's feed every night, irrespective of the date,
For days are a repetition for most other species,
Wake up, scrounge for food, and sleep in peace,
Choice is an illusion for most other species in life,
With survival a victory - alongside all the strife,
I wonder if we humans are spoilt, by our ability to choose,
To be confused in chasing a unicorn that's actually a moose.

—————————————————Downpourofwords

Footnote: *What is that one thing you could call as yours, that one thing which makes you feel at ease with Earth, on all fours? Our lives are comfortable, and no longer a battle of survival to exist, but an unending barrage of confusions that we find hard to resist.*

The world unknown

There's an unknown world everywhere,
Around us and in every place else,
That resides mostly in our sub-conscience,
Yet remains unappreciated, as a trivial presence,
Not by choice but often in a false pretense,
From an act of knowingly ignoring its existence.
It's a world that has its home in us people,
Between the tongue and the hearts so feeble.
It's a place where the thoughts can solemnly erupt,
Caressed by feelings that are weird & genuine, yet not be called corrupt,
At times it takes us on a ride between them stars,
From a world inside us, that thrives in the dark.
A dark spell that's cast upon by the human mind
Chained by rules, and inhibitions of every kind.
——————————————————Downpourofwords

Footnote: *The power of our sub-conscious mind that often flirts with our conscious and leaves its traces, it's very much underestimated. What can be a magical world of possibilities does also come with chains of inhibitions that can make lives akin to mere entities. Everything is from and after all, in the mind.*

Clones at the Beach

People of different kinds on the beach,
Some loitering around, some looking peach,
Some kids carve their imagination in the sands,
While some lay down for a mudpack from the sands,
Some brave-hearts surf like fishes on the waves,
While some laze around on beautiful colorful chairs,
Some spit out salty water coming out of the sea,
While some just sit watching the Sun and the deep blue sea,
People of different shapes and sizes come over to the beach,
Some with chiseled bodies with fitness lessons to teach,
Lessons for others who see abs as out of reach,
While some lay threadbare wanting to reverse nature's natural bleach,
Some sit or lay down with a book as a companion, to read,
While some enjoy the bliss in flying Seagulls wanting to feed,
Some sit there with a transfixed smile, watching their kids,
While some sit lost in deep thoughts about life and its dibs,
The strangest to me, are the ones lost in their phones,
Missing wonderful moments, resigned to being clones.

—————————————————Downpourofwords

Footnote: *A poem penned on a beach in Panama City, Florida. I wrote a poem about the ones who were lost in their phones instead of enjoying the beauty of the ocean, whilst being hooked myself to my laptop screen, writing away for a while, at the cost of looking myself, like a clone on the beach.*

Drifting in your lullaby

The presence of you in my mind,
Truth be told it's one of a kind,
As I draw a breath in, whilst seeing you smile,
I sense those seas swell, on them high tides,
I sense an angel inside of me preside,
Over a carnival of desires in my mind,
Where feelings play along like a trance,
Enacting love, chivalry, and a little romance,
At times when you are away from my sight,
I carry a torch, with its switch in my mind,
I turn it on to see those beautiful flashes,
Of you that I have eternally captured.
You are with me even when not with me,
I like to drift into spaces, in your unheard lullaby.
——————————————Downpourofwords

Footnote: *To love someone so much that their presence as well as their absence can make you go weak, in different ways, is Love. To feel the most hypnotic of tunes without the aid of any instrument, and to dance to those tunes ceremoniously, is Love.*

Who planted the deadly weeds?

I wonder what happened, why and when,
Since the first signs of human life began,
At what point did we alter our tracks,
To have come this car, to see more of cracks.
Was it an incident or a wayward deed?
That planted an ugly seed, of a deadly weed,
A weed that grew, feasting on inner darkness,
That's as much a part of us humans, as much as kindness.
A weed that grew over time, until conscience got clouded,
So much so that it seeped into actions, that got shrouded,
Till its roots entangled compassionate hearts, until cornered,
Right inside the hearts of the minds that it devoured,
I wonder when was it that learning to live and to evolve,
Turned into a game of divide & conquer, even dissolve,
The very virtues on which humanity once stood and evolved,
Are now replaced by hatred, envy, greed for life to be gnawed,
Making a home into the fabric of Society, that once happily stood,
On the same virtues of humanity, as brotherhood,
I see the world of today in a totally different light,
And I can't stop wondering, who and what caused this plight!
——————————————————Downpourofwords

Footnote: *The precipice at which we stand today is a sheet of thin ice which is melting away, with a ravaging mass of lava beneath, ready to spring upwards & engulf us all, if we do not change our minds, and more so our hearts. To change ourselves to be more compassionate, more considerate, more appreciative of another's good. To not be caught in petty battles that get us to where we once started, only feeling higher due to what we gathered, not acquired. What changed though, in the sands of time, and when?*

I don't like them scars

Lean on me, fall on me if you like,
I have grown my shoulders strong for such times,
For those nights that you feel are dreary and long,
When life's not so much a hopeful song.
Shed your tears, let them dry off on me,
They won't find a better place to be,
For there's an ocean of tears that I hide,
That I dry with hot air from hope, deep inside.
Lean on me and dispel all your fears,
The new ones or the clingy ones from years,
Rub your pain off on me and I will oblige,
Peeling it off your skin, I shall see you smile,
But as you decide to move away from me,
Watch your nails, I don't like them scars on me.
——————————————————Downpourofwords

Footnote: *To be there for someone in their times of need, to be gentle and kind, to be acceptant and mild, is also a service to humankind.*

Drifting away

I feel I am on a sail and drifting away,
Unraveling a new me in many ways,
Stupefied at times, awestruck other times,
At times playing hide and seek with nothing but time.
I see a glimpse of a mountain now and then,
With blinding flashes of the word 'WHEN',
Flashes in my mind that's always seeking answers,
To questions about life, love, purpose, kindness across invisible drawers,
Some answers lay inside me, some are outside,
Truth though, most questions are erased on the inside.
I see reality-a mean bitch though, binding humans in chains
Chains from things to do, worries of the past, writhing in pain,
I sail along until I see a few heartfelt smiles,
And I wonder how I catch that vibe, to spread it a thousand miles,
I tighten my grip on my sailboat wheel,
And drift along seeing more, taking it the way, it feels.

—————————————Downpourofwords

Footnote: *At times, don't we all see our mind wandering away into unknown territories, into lives of people we don't know, into the lives of people we know and into a contemplation of life in general?*

Page Not Found

'Page not found' glared back that screen,
On a page which had a million views, seen,
It was about a man who once fought,
A battle to outwit the unjust, and wonderfully lost.
His legend was not forgotten but was deftly wiped,
By the envious brigade who ruled every square mile.
But even those square miles had a jurisdiction,
To call their own realm, and gnaw in unison,
All he had done was listened often to his heart,
And in the larger scheme, played his worthwhile part,
And when his time came to finally depart,
He looked back and saw a masterpiece of an Art,
His fault, in this world was, despite all the dark,
He kept looking at everyone, as a piece of Art,
To finally realize, some pieces belong, only to the dark,
A monument carved on his name now stands tall,
The website's back live, and the haters look on, from behind a wall.

———————————————————Downpourofwords

Footnote: *A poetic rendition of a thought on the many people who picked up on a cause, made it a part of their own, battled a thousand odds & left behind a legacy, to then be ridiculed, judged and had traces of their work taken off by the ones not powerful but ones who held the authority at that point in time.*

Wake up, not as me?

What if I woke up one morning?
Shrunk in size, looking miniscule & minimalistic,
To see myself as such, with a look of surprise,
To be astonished who ate away the rest of my human size,
To then try and speak a word or two, to try,
Only to hear a buzz that I faintly recognize,
As something annoying from when I was big,
A fly or a buzz, how did I end up in this gig?
And as I raise my hands, erm wait, I see wings,
To see myself fly off them box springs,
And to see the world in an entirely new dimension,
A view deeper, bigger yet narrow, all in unison.
To leave me in a state of heightened delirium,
And be happy to be flapping wings to see newer horizons.
Which way would I then fly I wonder?
Into those plains ever so springy green,
Or into the woods with an alternate sky in green,
Or into the tantalizing humid air of the deep blue seas,
Or would I fly into the lives of the ones in need,
Even as a fly, I wouldn't be lured just by greed.

——————————————————-Downpourofwords

Footnote: *I think one of the most wished for acts in life is the ability to fly. To feel free to soar into the skies, flapping one's wings, it has been an inspiration for many a inventions and literary pieced being penned on the topic. This poem is about a hypothetical scenario of waking up one day, as a fly.*

A hopeful Song

I am a wanderer in the wilderness of the woods,
Having packed light, having unloaded some goods,
For when I wander in these unknown trails or set out on sails,
There's not much room in my mind, to sit and wail,
For there are demons I carry along, on my tail,
They are the clingy clingers; they latch on to any of my waywardly sails.
They lure me at time by their sweetened words,
That in time turn into glistening swords,
They know to turn the tides towards an abyss,
If only I fall prey to their flattery and their deadly kiss.
Walking or sailing this way to me, seems like a perfect song,
For even if I feel withdrawn at times, I push along,
And I know when I walk whilst carrying them on my back,
It wouldn't take much for them, to send me off my track.
Once when resting under a banyan tree, I heard some footsteps behind,
Of someone invisible deciding to acknowledge my guile,
And soon there's a chorus of voices saying, *'Let's keep going on'*,
It fills my air with hope, and I sit to write a Hopeful Song.
—————————————————Downpourofwords

Footnote: *At times when you know that path you have set about in your mind and in your life is right, the universe is bound to give you assurances that seem whimsical to believe in. At times you end up questioning your own sanity in believing in such things, yet when you look back, it was such moments as well that played a part in getting you to where you stand, today.*

Risk free acts

A random chatter, or a random laughter,
Breaking the silence sometimes, is all that matters,
And the fact is, it's not the deeds not done,
But rather the things felt, but the words left unspoken,
That leave behind an insurmountable mountain so big,
For you to then stand and wonder, to climb or dig?
The mind though is an unchartered ocean on its own,
In a conundrum on what to say, what to leave hidden,
Ah that question, we all know, is a tough one,
But within us is where all answers find their reasons,
Stand as is, or go along with those words of yours,
And turn them into acts that bring along a smile or maybe wipe a tear,
For in such acts, there is happiness and not much of risk,
Of being hurt, betrayed, or be left walking with a stick.

————————————————Downpourofwords

Footnote: *An average human speaks 7000 to 20000 words in a day. And an average of 50000+ thoughts cross our minds in a day. How many of those thoughts & feelings find their way out as words? For whatever reason, we do not say everything we feel, believe in, in our day to day lives. Words that put someone in a better place than they were before they heard your words, are what I call as words uttered as risk free acts.*

In the timeless times

If ever there is a time,
It is now. This very moment.
To grab what's yours,
Or pull those threads,
That you carelessly tossed,
Many a times in the past.
Go on now, grab those shoes,
And head on out to where you belong.
For there's no song without music,
There's no action in just dreaming,
Like there is, in the act of doing.
Time is timeless for one and all,
Very little differentiates who stands tall,
And who has a crashing fall.
—————————————————Downpourofwords

Footnote: *I barely pen poems that do not rhyme. This is one of those out of the comfort zone attempts at penning a poem differently.*

On the move

I thought it was enough to be on the move,
So long as I unraveled truths every-time new,
And the farther I moved on my inside and the outside,
One glaring truth, it stood the test of times.
It's a simple fact that whatever we pursue,
Steers our ride towards it, with every move,
Not any move but the ones that are aligned,
To the blissful abode where our dreams reside,
And at times when the legs do get tired,
Just believe and know it's just another time to bide,
And you shall again be on your spunky little ride,
Piercing through howling winds, smiling wide.
It's a flickering game, being on the move,
Inch by inch, weaving your life story afresh anew,
Every new day, is in essence a chance to rightfully move,
Towards anything that we really want, to come true.

——————————————Downpourofwords

Footnote: *"Try, Try, Try till you succeed", "Baby steps to success", do those phrases ring a bell? There is no secret to success, unless you are extremely lucky, and luck doesn't stick around for long unless there is true worth. A way to our dreams is often in the million times we move ahead in alignment with our goals, day in day out.*

Ain't that bad

Isn't it mildly true that every one of us,
Have those million-dollar dreams that reside in us,
Not as a firm belief, but rather as a timid wish,
In most cases, just to know how it really feels.
But deep down inside there's an eye,
Oblivious to occurrences on the outside,
It's where all the mysteries & the good things reside,
It's a place where the dreams get tried.
Not blind are those eyes wishing for a dollar dream,
For that's how happiness was always shown & seen,
Not more so on the inside, but shown vehemently on the outside,
In media, news, debates & most of them movies alike,
To imagine oneself being a millionaire one time,
And to try & see what else is it that's driven inside,
Is an act we all need to engage in, to think & dwell,
For life isn't enough just with money, it's also something else,
To wish isn't a bad thing, but to not question is bad,
A chat with oneself, once in a while, ain't that bad
——————————————Downpourofwords

Footnote: *Imagine yourself waking up as a millionaire with money no longer one of your worries. How does that feel? Blissful of course. Imagine your life as that a few days, weeks, months and imagine one dreary day waking up and feeling something missing. Money isn't all that we need in life.*

Fragrance of hope

Those dark clouds that hovered in the sky,
Are passing now, as I can see those birds fly,
Those moments of anguish are gone now,
Like the Sun beating down on melting snow.
Those lost guardian angels are back now,
Like spring after a winter, stormy & cold,
Those moments of being lost are long gone,
Like the fear demon chased by affirmative humdrums.
I open my secret chest of perfumes, those of life,
And pick a can of hope, spray it where I like,
And as I swivel in its mesmerizing fragrance,
I let that moment linger, feel its essence,
And then I trod on hopeful, yet well aware,
Next dark cloud might well be on its way.

——————————————————Downpourofwords

Footnote: *We all have an intellect, an ability to reflect, to make sense of our present, our pasts and the way we are headed into our future. We all have positive thoughts, our fears, our bag of worries and our bagful of assurances alongside a bagful of wishes that we carry. And all of these are invisible entities that reside in our mind. What differentiates some who surge ahead from the ones who feel stuck in life? It's what you pluck from your mind more often.*

The night wagoner's

Aren't a certain breed of us night dwellers,
When we lay motionless at night, in far off corners,
While resting in presence, but not in essence,
Drifting in thoughts and their flirtatious presence,
Often categorized as being them insomniacs,
But we are people who are in love with the silent dark.
It's in the dark that we find a piece of time,
To let go off life's shackles, & slowly unwind,
For being lost in thoughts is also an unappreciated gift,
It's a way into our minds, in letting our thoughts drift,
Just like every day we face isn't really a charm,
So isn't every night calm & blissfully warm,
Yet being lost in thoughts at night feels like a norm,
For the silence of the night fosters a thoughtful swarm,
And every time the night wagon, it whistles & comes on,
We are travelers who are waiting to just hop on.
————————————Downpourofwords

Footnote: *I wonder at times if some of us are dwellers of the dark or explorers of the dawn or a mix of both. This poem explores the essence of being someone who has found a meaning to thoughtful thoughts in the presence of the dark.*

What's what to you?

To a photographer, every face is a model,
To a writer, every face is a story untold,
To a doctor, every grimace is a certain vein,
To a psychiatrist, everyone's almost sane,
To an actor, every other person is a character,
To a mason, every shape is a sculpture,
To a poet, every event is an inspiration,
To a musician, every sound is an introduction,
To a carpenter, every piece of wood is a to be Art,
To a Painter, every scene is an image apart,
To a director, every incident a possible plot,
To an athlete, every day is worth a walk,
To the creator, every life is an unseen evolution,
To a believer, every moment is a step to retribution.

—————————————————Downpourofwords

Footnote: *There's always something which has way more dimensions to it than other things. To visualize something differently than what others visualize it as, is what differentiates what interests us.* And it is in things that we see in more ways than one, that we can usually excel. *Food for thought for the youngsters to try & make sense of what to be, in life.*

Rainy signs

On those distant gloomy skies,
In between the intermittent lightning strikes,
Accompanied by thunder, rumbling left and right,
A rainy thought like a lightning, struck my mind.
While we live down here in our comfy lairs,
What goes on in those skies up there,
If nothing else, could the rains & thunder be a sign,
To look up there for once, into the high skies,
And for a moment forget, petty strife's & false pride,
Or the unending list of worries of a journey called life,
To look down from up above & see an opportunity called life,
To know we all are humans, regardless of tribe,
To be kind at heart, not play games or guiles,
To try make a difference, in someone's life,
To try and spread a few heartfelt smiles,
If nothing else, be lost watching the rains, and admire.

—————————————————————————————Downpourofwords

Footnote: *What separates us down below here, is what we have separated ourselves as. We have labels, sects, trades, notions, beliefs, ideologies, race, religion, jobs, statuses that differentiate us. But from up above in those skies, if we look down on Mother Earth and know there is a massive congregation of a possibility called life, all that's visible at that altitude are differences we carry as different species, not what we carry within our species.*

A day in the woods

Some hay I carry, in my backpack,
The toothpaste I carry, in my zip lock,
The fish food I carry, in my backpack,
The air bag I carry, on my shoulder strap,
A slingshot I carry, in my backpack,
A book & a laptop I carry, in my messenger bag,
A few bottles of water I carry, in my backpack,
A pouch of dry fruits neatly wrapped.
Is all that I need for a walk in the woods,
Everything I carry is for something solemnly good.
The hay I carry, is for the white sheep,
The fish food is for the cute little fish,
The slingshot so the rabbits can feed,
The laptop for the moments my thoughts call out in need,
The airbag for resting a bit, if there's a need,
The dry fruits for survival, if I get lost indeed,
That's all I need I think, for a day in the woods,
At times nature is a way to feel at peace, feel good.
————————————————————Downpourofwords

Footnote: *A poetic rendition of the bliss in spending time with nature, & with other life, as a means to experience some moments in a different sense, that how we experience it for most of our lives. Side note - Safety & preparation is a necessary aspect to consider too while venturing out into the woods.*

Untimely whims

The frailties of your frivolous thoughts,
Were evident in a way, right from the start,
Maybe I was lost, searching for a spot,
To rest a while, from my thoughts playing riot,
And from rains that somehow didn't seem to stop,
Kept following me whichever way I walked,
In that moment that I found your lonesome raft,
On which you sat alone, & wickedly laughed,
I saw the glitter of the gold & diamond you wore,
Must have slayed many a men, right through their cores,
Didn't entice me that much, as I rarely get swept,
Just by the flair on the outside, & your insides unkept,
I chose the cold waters instead & I went for a swim,
Away from your raft and your guile & your untimely whims.

——————————————————Downpourofwords

Footnote: *The choices we make & the many diversions we take, also end up defining us as a person. What's enticing isn't always inspiring.*

Innocent till proven guilty

Forgive me will you, for I did not hear,
What you just rattled on, for about an hour,
It isn't about me having a malfunctioning ear,
Or a matter of you becoming not so dear,
It's just a simple liking in my heart, if it matters,
I like looking at you, more than your incessant chatter.
At times when I look at you, all I do is wander,
Into unknown realms, far across and yonder,
Where it's me and you, in the company of our thoughts,
At time I see a cloud of Love with the piercing darts,
With the breeze of beautiful thoughts gushing in my ears,
Tell me how can I listen, or be able to hear?
The words from your soothing voice, I let them go on,
Innocent till proven guilty, I keep looking on.

——————————————————————Downpourofwords

Footnote: *To be drawn by someone's voice, eyes, gestures and be lost in a way that nonchalantly feels like ignorance at face value, can also be a way of feeling love, admiration.*

Just to giggle

A friend in this lane, a friend in that lane,
Taking a walk without being noticed, was always in vain,
For one of them would see me walking straight,
And whistle at me, egging me to come their way,
To talk about what time is it that we shall play,
Even if it was a ritual, the same time every day.
But behind that whistle was a hidden intent,
A heartfelt yet harmless one, something nonchalant,
From friends who would do anything to mingle,
No invites, no Dutch checks, just to huddle up & giggle,
Times like that are also what make us feel real,
If life's a carnival, friends add that color, are the real deal,
In simple gestures of life, does real magic rest,
Without few close buds, won't life be an impossible test?
——————————————————Downpourofwords

Footnote: *Friendship is a relation that is often overshadowed by the attention that Love, Motherhood, Fatherhood, Sibling bonds receive. No judgments there but there are moments in life which have their true meaning only with friends with whom you yearn to spend time with.*

Momentous life

Life is potpourri of a million little moments,
Some memorable, others worth a lament,
Some sweeter than honey, some bitter,
Most so trivial, they aren't remembered,
Some spent in deep thought, some lost,
Some spent daydreaming, ruing the past,
Some so impactful, they leave a mark,
Some so vengeful, leaving one lurching in the dark,
Some so insightful, dispelling the doubts,
Some so hurtful, carrying along dark clouds,
Life is a two-sided coin, it seems short for once,
Yet other times, feels longer than marathons,
In between all this, life is also an experiential joy ride,
If lived wholeheartedly, there's a chance of walking with pride.
——————————————Downpourofwords

Footnote: *What is Life? There must be a thousand definitions of what life is and here's another attempt at defining what this magnanimous opportunity called life is.*

It is, what it is

It is really what it is,
And will be so, if left as is,
For it likes to be at ease,
That's where it sees a need,
A need to be often validated,
Often repeatedly recalibrated,
In one's own mind, that's usually cluttered,
Often in search of an adulation, something that matters,
It can push aside even a belief that's strong,
Yet one side of us, it still eggs on,
To look and validate oneself,
Not through other's clouded lenses,
But in one's own intellect & senses,
To look inside through one's own lenses,
A strand of doubt, is all it takes,
To really let something be - as it is.
—————————————Downpourofwords

Footnote: *We all deal with lethargy in life. Often times the act of being lethargic is associated to physical inactivity. However, lethargy is more deadly when it is lethargy of one's own mind. Not by choice but by doubts & fears created by external factors which we did not inherit when we were born. Yet they end up being so powerful that they turn even the most vibrant of minds to be caught up being lethargic.*

Abyss-mile deep

Entrenched in those wily self-doubts,
Aren't we all a herd of trapped souls,
The belief in us was, and will always be there,
Yearning for that gush of fresh air,
For in the darkness when the chains are on,
There's also a deadly silence, and no songs,
The clutter from the chains it adds on,
To the apathy, that knows nothing but to cling on,
And in a simple act of conformance, unsought,
Lives get lived without a second thought.
A deadly lullaby it is, quite unbecoming,
Is that plunge driven by a doubt filled leap?
Into an abyss that runs many a mile deep,
Where no sounds get heard, even when you weep.
————————————————Downpourofwords

Footnote: *It is not uncommon these days to know someone who is depressed or is being treated for depression. The list has always been there but it's growing in treacherous ways. This poem explores the pangs of depression & the feeling of being caught up, tied down despite having a mighty belief in oneself & one's abilities.*

A battle Royale undone

I once fought a lonely battle in my heart,
Where inhibitions, they played a big part,
A battle between me and my inner Art,
I was lost, not knowing where to start.
Maybe I was a con, playing a blinding part,
In knowing and not knowing what lacked,
And what I was doing wasn't really enough,
Letting words erupt and silently die off,
Not caring to pick and nurture them in time,
Or try to contemplate or make them rhyme,
But then I began a blind journey with my Art,
Letting words out, the way they came out,
I feel better for having played a little part,
In respecting this presence inside me, my Art.
————————————Downpourofwords

Footnote: *There is no cure to a writer's block. There is no other way than to pen those thoughts that need to be penned. The process of creating something in itself is a beautiful experience.*

What's different today?

Those first few steps of my return run,
Boy let me tell you they ain't no fun,
For even before I head out the front door,
I hear a humdrum of inhibitions inside me starting to roar,
It's in such moments filled with doubt though,
That the seeds of the right kind are sown,
Easier said than done, I know the pains,
And so, I planned, invented a little mind game.
I named the game as '*what's different today?*'
It's not fully fair, but then it's also fair,
I walk out getting my mind prepared,
To see if I shall see something different,
Even in the same trails that I daily tread,
And most times it works, shakes the mind off its dread,
And by the time I notice a difference for the day,
I am far away into those repetitive trails.
——————————————————Downpourofwords

Footnote: *One of the best gifts given to us is the power of intellect. With it, many a boulder in life's path have been crushed in the past & will continue to be taken out. One such gift is also the fact that we can trick our minds into doing certain difficult things. Here's a poem about how I devised a way to trick my mind into going out for walks or runs, more often.*

A proposal of Love - silenced

There was anguish all around the place,
A frown reminiscent of a painful farce,
That seemed to have started to cool off,
Only on the outside, while the insides were still hot,
He wasn't in his senses, but he walked right in,
The happiness in those faces, hard not to be seen,
To him, it was an act of vengeance that he sought,
Things were to be straightened, here on out,
He hadn't seen a known face till now, in the dark,
He kept lurking in the shadows, breathing hard,
There was a raging fire in his every breath,
And beneath his tucked shirt, he carried a form of death,
It erupted, left behind a shocking death,
Of a stranger in a crowd contemplating a proposal of love that weekend,
An innocent life, one of possible essence had been shot,
Victim to a trigger of an aimless, angry gunshot.

—————————————Downpourofwords

Footnote: *A poetic rendition of the inexplicable shootouts that occur in these times, often occurring due to mental illnesses on part of the perpetrators.*

Eyes around

The eyes I see in these phases of life,
Make me wonder, what secrets they hide?
For sometimes what's visible to the naked eyes,
That can't be taken at face value, for eyes do hide,
Some eyes, I call them the rising tides,
For they gleam with abundance & life,
Some eyes, I call them hurtful smiles,
For they smile even with tears inside,
Some eyes, I call them wicked bears,
They stop at nothing, not even tears,
Some eyes I call them a castle of deceit,
They measure everything by what they receive,
Some eyes, I call them the horny mules,
For they see one emotion, in every single drool.
Billions of eyes all around, walking along,
Each humming a song or trying to right some wrong.
—————————————Downpourofwords

Footnote: *The eyes that we see in our everyday lives, each have a story of their own. It is no longer easy to read the look in someone's eyes at face value, for there's many a skills acquired as part of evolution & through information, that there's more caution to be exercised even in the simplest of things we see. Quoting the famous phrase "There's always more to it than what meets the eye".*

A duel with life

Hang on to me with all you got,
For I plan be turn into a juggernaut,
With you along, I shall wildly soar,
Into the skies amidst your uproar,
And when I down my gear a few notches,
Hold on tight in that descent, we are downing paces,
For then on for a few beautiful miles,
We shall smoothly traverse, I want to see just smiles,
We can laugh a bit, talk a little more,
About now, how, all that beautiful folklore,
A little later, I shall sound a blaring horn,
It's your cue to gently nod and hop off,
For I would have taken you from a place of unrest,
To a better place using my word flight, at its best,
For then on the flight will only be mine,
Fires lay ahead and I got a duel with life.

—Downpourofwords

Footnote: *One of the reasons I write is because I have always believed that words can be a beautiful reason to feeling better. This is as is evident when we listen to music & let those sounds and words resonate with us, influence us & inspire us. This poem is about a Poet's wish to take the readers on a hope filled ride & to leave them at a better place than where they started at, & to then continue on my sojourn alone, then on.*

A blurry painting

Even a look at those deep blue skies,
Can resemble a gloomy movie at times,
Or when looking at a complete family, in smiles,
Their three generations enjoying a happy tide,
I yearn to have ears like a wolf at the time,
To live a moment listening to their jibes,
But then I realize I got to move on,
Whoever pauses a playing favorite song?
I walk along carrying that little image,
Of the smiles and I turn it into a trace,
For me to try and paint a portrait of my own,
Even if it means ending up with a face forlorn,
And in collecting happy moments of others as images,
I shall capture moments in words, that to me, are mirages,
The yearning to be in the thick of it all,
Wouldn't be a reason for me to pause or take a fall.

——————————————————Downpourofwords

Footnote: *At times, watching happy times of others can be a feeling of happiness or a moment of sadness, whichever way you take it. It is impossible to turn a blind eye to things that we miss in our lives. Yet there's always a silver lining in life, to try & turn such moments into something good.*

Grab that moon

When I look back at our times together and wonder,
What do you think I often remember?
For there were a million moments that we spent,
Under the sun, the ceiling, & the places we went.
It's a movie of sorts that I see in action,
I wonder if all that was a myth or was it fiction?
For what we are now, it feels beyond imagination,
And it's true that everything seldom has an explanation.
The movie though it runs at 8x for a pace,
Pausing only to show the pertinent traces,
Where you and me, traversed out of our worldly existence,
Both in good and bad, there was an essence,
The now feels calmer now, I'm walking on,
And wish for you, a good life and that moon.
————————————————Downpourofwords

Footnote: *Relationships in life are a means for our own growth in more ways than one. And in a world where break-ups are looked upon mostly as hurtful separations, often followed up by words or acts of vengeance, does it make sense to take a step back & reflect on the good times & carry them forward as memories, and still wish well for the ones separated?*

Year 2060

The sneaky reverses, and hand gestures,
The skillful maneuvers, and missed turns,
The screeching tires, the hearts on fire,
The sense of control, while hearing a choir,
And matching the tempo of the drive,
In random moments of music coming alive,
That intentional act of getting really lost,
That sense of planning time for a drive, quite an Art,
Aren't all these that make driving feel, right?
Having humane control of where we go now feels alright.
Driving is an act that holds its own as a chore,
A chore with hidden beauty only if explored,
All this will soon be gone or stay as folklore,
When the machines take over the roads, while we can snore,
For we shall all be zombies inside our cars,
Handing off our instincts to technology raising the bar,
The discipline on the roads will be quite high,
While some older women & men veer out of their windows & sigh.

—————————————————Downpourofwords

Footnote: *To some, driving is a chore or just a means to reach from point A to point B. For some, driving is an Art, a way of connecting with oneself through the act of driving whilst being in control. A futuristic poem written with the people who love driving now, in first person & how they would take the fact that all cars at some point will be AI driven.*

Little by little

Are we all victims of our own mind?
Scavenging inside for answers to find,
Like a raging fire, the questions do spread,
Throbbing often times, inkling a feeling of dread,
And there's always a question about daily bread,
Which often binds us to a life to be led.
In a world where money talks bolder,
More than the words and actions that really matter,
The voices of the right kind do get lost in oblivion,
As worthy little souls get coerced into submission,
If only there was a better way to hop on,
Onto a ride where choice isn't an option,
Is it too late to redesign little by little?
Rearranging society and to be it more on mettle.

—————————————————Downpourofwords

Footnote: *If there's a massive worldwide survey on how many people are really in love with their jobs, it wouldn't be a startling discovery to see more than 50% of the responses being in the negative. The way the society is structured, the need to earn one's bread & support a shelter are what drive what people do, most of the times. Is there something that could be done to tilt the scales & make it easier for people to align to their passions in more numbers?*

Tomfoolery of thoughts

A charter flown into an unknown territory,
Or a stumble into unchartered territory,
A playful gang full of tomfoolery,
Or a playful tomfoolery on a gang,
A sail into a soulful ensemble of melodies,
Or a tune transforming into a soulful melody,
A righteous fighting for that victory,
Or a righteous victory dispelling parity,
A treacherous way of acting insanely,
Or a treacherous act defying sanity,
A love-filled expression in the air,
Or love-filled air, hearts out of despair,
A lived spent more un-lived than lived,
Or the un-lived lives consuming the living dead?
—————————————Downpourofwords

Footnote: *The poem is what it says it is. A tomfoolery of contradicting polarities of acts, thoughts & meanings, so to speak.*

The place you sent me to

I went to the place that you sent me to,
I was looking for the sun, I landed in snow,
I was looking for the people, I found hollows,
I was looking for the mountains, I found shallows,
I was looking for some warmth, I turned yellow,
Where instead of finding an answer, I felt low,
Where instead of finding water, I found banter,
Where instead of finding solace, I found farce,
Now I get a thought, you did put me through a lot,
But then, didn't I carve a hole, tear my way out?
I have learned an ocean from where you once sent me,
Now is my time, for you helped me find me.
I see now in your alleys, a bigger demon lurks,
He's unmistakably mean, waits to return all the perks,
I wish the truth had for once, been told in my face,
At least I would know, I'd be fighting someone with Grace.
——————————————————Downpourofwords

Footnote: *In hindsight, the people who act mean to us, and undeservingly so, end up being the biggest lessons that our lives need. In hindsight, if not for certain people being mean, certain events going haywire, is a missed opportunity to unleashing that inner fire, the humane desire.*

A winner-less battle

There's a strange way that my mind works,
And being weird has its own little perks,
For even on a journey full of unforeseen bumps,
A jovial traveler often lets his heart jump.

I had thought my mind was just another mind,
Until I dwelled deep inside to then find,
That most answers to my questions, did solemnly reside,
Inside the enclosures of my human mind.

A little coercing, a little fist fight maybe,
When channeled though, acts like a naive baby,
It can't be tamed though, only honed a little,
For the worldly chains we try with, are frail & brittle.

It's a battle where the winner is only one,
And the demons are all inside, outside none,
Battle them within, until one by one they seem gone.
And that spirited fight inside the mind, it carries on.
——————————————Downpourofwords

Footnote: *The power of the human mind is often underestimated.
Look within for that's where most of the answers we see, reside.*

Less to vent

The pebbles we collected on the shores,
The T-shirt's that we brought at the seaside store,
The wind chimes that we collected like fools,
Not to be hoisted, rather hung aloof,
The clueless menus that we ate out of,
The exits that we kept missing on the roads,
The stones that we made to hop on the waters,
Aren't those the little things that really mattered?

The mad rush for a movie fucked up,
Leaving us laughing on how it turned out,
The moments that we gathered unnoticed,
They happened with ease, bereft of practice,
And some of those didn't even make sense,
But they left behind a lingering presence of essence.
When I am drifting along in those moments that we spent,
I know I have lived well & have a lot less to vent.
————————————————————Downpourofwords

Footnote: *It's not often that the bigger much awaited moments in life that stay with us, as memories. Maybe some. But life & the memories we make, the ones we bake, & when the end comes, the moments that we gracefully carry & take, are little moments of joy, little gestures of life.*

Waits of life

Is life filled with a million moments,
Or rather a million unnerving currents?
Is it a mixture of all the above, in tandem?
Swiveled into existence in our lives, at random?
From even a wait, to be able to speak,
To waiting to speak when able, but thoughts going weak,
From a wait to get onto a school bus,
To waiting for school after an exodus,
From an eternal wait of that return smile,
To waiting for a reply on a blinking screen, at night,
From waiting to grow up to do bigger things,
To waiting for miracles to let go off what clings,
The momentous waits I know, shall never cease,
It's unto us I think, to wait in unrest or to carry on, in peace.

————————————————Downpourofwords

Footnote: *Aren't we all waiting for something in life? That bigger paycheck, that special someone, that dream vacation, that mansion of a house, that fighting for a cause, that opportunity to hear an applause? The waits of life to me it seems, shall never end. It's how we wade through them smiling, around every bend, that defines where we shall one day, finally end.*

The favorites game

"What is your favorite game"? she asked,
One where I get to win, with no fairness lost,
"What is your favorite place?" she asked,
One with no fear, of getting lost,
"What is your favorite hobby?" she asked,
One without drudgery, lurking in the dark,
"What is your favorite color?" she asked,
One which dispels hope, in a life so stark,
"What is your favorite possession?" she asked,
Some memories from my reminiscent past,
"What is your favorite obsession?" she asked,
Being able to ignite, & spread that spark,
She had had enough, she took an exit march,
Vanished like an empty shadow, in the dark.
—————————————————————Downpourofwords

Footnote: *What you sometimes seek, and in the end what you reap,*
is also defined by the thoughts on the other end, mighty, or meek.

Silent surfers

The look that I see in some eyes,
It clearly shows what they hide inside,
I ain't a surfer but I've been on mighty tides,
I have seen those surges where the fears reside.
And whilst there, I built a little bond,
In company of a few who liked to push hard,
And in those moments spent riding along,
We hummed a little, made our own whacky songs.
There was something in the air, & it spread,
Calmed the sweaty nerves, as well erased that dread,
It was a moment of inspiration from that extra push,
It transformed into a beautiful hazy mist, it went aloof,
The aroma in the air did the rest and it poured,
A shower of inspiration, and magic occurred.

—————————————Downpourofwords

Footnote: *Oftentimes, what we can or cannot do is dependent on the kind of people we surround ourselves with. If there is an amalgamation of rightful intent, with those around who have positive thoughts-potent, the end result is nothing else, but an ambience filled with possibilities, to upturn realities.*

A forever new beginning

When the world around you stops making sense,
It's easy to fall prey, to a false pretense,
For there are millions out there, raking in steps,
In the same state every day, in thinking faking helps.
But what if they fake a while and then move on,
And I stay stuck in an abyss I created on my own?
It's easy to be preyed on than to give in,
In such a play, there are certainly no battles to win.

That's when it strikes me, out of the blue,
People often, can be compared to a sticky glue,
To look into, to derive from, or to bind for good,
No point ruing a sequence of "I Could",
More pertinent than observing is the act of noticing, then imbibing,
What I should be, what I shouldn't be, in living,
And to learn even from good & the bad, to keep moving,
It's the trait that shall mean to you, a forever new beginning.
—————————————————Downpourofwords

Footnote: *The world & the people we have around us are overtly smart. Information is available in abundance. Everyone can learn as much as they seek, even if the souls weep, and are inherently weak. How do you tell from a healthy soul from a wealthy soul? By observing deeper. There's something that will usually give way. And when you realize the truth, learn from it. It is really unto us to choose what to be, through what we notice, imbibe & also unto us to choose what how we shouldn't be through what we notice & imbibe.*

A technical snag

He walked into a box-shaped piece of Art,
A building standing tall, in pitch black,
A yellow halo emanated from the corners,
Crafted elegantly with glossy borders,
The building was built for miracles,
To try and break those binding shackles,
Not from nature, nor from the forces outside,
But the ones that reside deep within us, inside.
It was designed to act as a black hole,
It would rake in all negative vibes from ones onboard,
To flush out a human who would walk in with a heart cold,
And walk out to live life more openly, being just & bold,
A weird guy who went in, with a gruesome past,
Came out with explosions behind his back,
—————————————Downpourofwords

Footnote: *A paradoxical way of looking at human emotions. If humankind were to make a technology that could try & take away pain, suffering & the cold in a human's heart, would it be able to check the boxes against someone with a past full of scars & hurt? Healing is often advised to those in pain as if it is a pill to pop whilst the reality is that healing is a process & takes its own time.*

A blob called Hope

In moments when we stare into silence,
Yearning a moment of a fleeting presence,
Of an unworldly and mysterious existence,
Of a feeling of deeper resemblance,
Of something that knows what's cooking,
Inside that heart that just goes on beating,
That something is a potion called hope,
A blob of energy that runs amok,
It's made of a flirty heart that hops along,
To anyone embracing it with open arms,
Hard to latch onto, its best left to travel,
But in silent moments, it rests in us for revival,
With a heartfelt outreach, it rides along,
Until it finds another arm to wrap around.

—————————————————Downpourofwords

Footnote: *What is life, if anything, without hope? Yet at times, it's very hard to feel hopeful & other times we find ourselves brimming with hope that carries us over into those dreamlands. Is there a perfect solution to feeling hopeful all the time? Probably not. However, looking back at our lives, at our most hopeless moments & in contemplating on how we came out of it, bruised but not broken, is an often-ignored power that we all have. Our pasts carry the power at times, to take us forward.*

Dancers in the dark

Hold on, oh my needy heart,
For what you are about to ask,
Will have implications rather stark,
And a possible plunge into the abysmal dark,
Or a lovely stroll in a mystical park,
If all the wheels do align alright, hit their mark.

All I see you doing, is to eternally beat,
Leaving me here alone, to then face the heat,
From the actions that I perform, in your wake,
That I innocently act upon, for your sake.

And most times I do so, not thinking twice,
For to me, you would never spin a vice,
Hang in there, be yourself, & we shall play our part,
Like foot tapping dancers invisible, in the dark.

—————————————————————Downpourofwords

Footnote: *The heart is technically a beating organ in our body. Yet we are surrounded by feelings, aplenty. And driven by it to act upon feelings, incessantly. A poetic rendition of a heart & the acts we blindly dive into at times, like dancers in the dark.*

Fear of unseen unknown

The words that you effortlessly speak,
They love to run around and sneak,
Into crevices on my inside, the ones real deep,
Where demons of mine, they lay asleep,
It's not a fear of those being known,
But rather the fear of the unseen unknown,
That makes me stop you in your tracks,
To not try and peep inside my cracks,
For I have now wandered too far along,
To be held back by a sodomizing song.
I like your words for when they ring,
Like the sounds of nature, blissfully resonating,
But some waters are best left not entered,
And does knowing everything, does it to you matter?
——————————————Downpourofwords

Footnote: *There are parts of me deep within that belong to me. In a way, they cling onto me. And we all carry parts of us out in the open & on the inside. It's in our insides that a lot of who we are, what we feel, & that essence of us, that reside. To know a person from the inside, it can be an altogether different ride.*

Age like fine wine

The wrinkles on your flawless skin,
Show how much of a beauty you have been,
For this way, at this age, this way to be seen,
How good to yourself you have you been?
It's amazing, for since when is life kind?
Dispelling all beings into a crawling twine,
And yet you stand there, & eloquently shine,
In your pristine beauty, despite having bid your time,
And to stand there, amidst a sea of adrenaline,
Holding your own, in aging like fine wine,
If beauty was a sham, its within that lurks the glam,
That look of pride you carry, it shines back with a bang,
Without a word spoken, you do tell a beautiful tale,
Despite all that you went through, the joys & the pains.

———————————————Downpourofwords

Footnote: *Don't we all come across a 50+ year woman who has hung onto herself internally & externally, in ways beautifully? And to be that way despite the fact that being a woman isn't easy, is a testimony to upholding one's identity, amidst life, and all of its parities & disparities. Age like fine wine is a rendition applauding all such women out there.*

A birth right

What if all the animals in the world,
Developed their own secret Morse code,
Start to tag along like one common herd,
And through the cryptic signals for humans, unheard,
Conjure up a blueprint of a master plan,
To gain back some space, & to call it their own,
For we humans have left no stone unturned,
In pushing them to mere beings, rather outgunned,
What would a sea of animals, the ones wild and mild?
Walking with fiery eyes, all side by side,
Turn up at our doors and ask for their rights,
Would we give in or end it with a fight?
Even if we win, would that be a deed alright?
Co-habitation isn't a fight, it's everyone's birth right.

———————————————————————————————————————Downpourofwords

Footnote: *A hypothetical thought on what would happen if all the animals we treat as inferior to us today, due to the shortcomings of the mind that we have been blessed with, decide to unite & ask for their space on this Earth? How would we react as humans, to such an eventuality?*

If Artists ruled

If the world were to be ruled by Artists,
Would there be any glaring twists?
Who would then define the boundaries,
When none exist inside those minds,
Would we then use unicorns as our rides?
Or nudge one another whilst flying on broom rides,
Would there be a universal human union?
A way to speak out together in unison,
Or would there be a chaos filled life,
Where misled dreams burn many a human pyre?
Would the issues of today be any different?
Or we would still straddle on in life, being ignorant?
Would the world then be a better place to be?
With dreams on higher pedestals, like they ought to be?
Would the world need some order, or an Artistic disorder?
Or should we let Art be Art, can our decisions be any bolder?
————————————————Downpourofwords

Footnote: *How many instances have we seen of an Artistic leader? If the rungs of society were to be re-laid with Artists having more of a say in administration & for that matter all aspects of life, how would the world then be? Would it be a better place or a place of chaos from an Artist's free will?*

Pedestal down beneath

I want to finish on a pedestal one day,
One that wouldn't be high up in the sky,
Rather down on the ground beneath,
Where I see some hearts that tremble, & weep,
For more than the shine in those stars,
I look for solace amongst them scars,
I wear a crown of nature made in green,
I dwell into spaces often new, unseen,
The pedestal shall have steps leading down,
Into an aura filled with acceptance, multifold,
Acceptance of being just the humankind,
Them frivolous differences not enough to bind,
To then uphold a few ailing hearts, to get them to try,
To be their best, in rising higher, to fly,
The pedestal though stumbles right now, with imbalance,
From intentions that collude a blissful existence.

—————————————Downpourofwords

Footnote: *Some find their solace in joy, some in adventure, some in misdemeanor, some in success & grandeur. Some like me also find a solace in finding beaten up hearts & then in taking them higher.*

Watch the sun go down

As the sun goes down, yet one more time,
Let there be a freedom, bereft of any binds,
Where you and me, dispel notions in kind,
And find a restful place to solemnly unwind.
A place not elsewhere, but inside our minds,
Where magic comes to life, as our thoughts collide,
And in that camaraderie of highflying thoughts,
There shall be untwining of insipid knots,
Having us bound, & broken into little parts,
At times feeling a pinch, like harmless frivolous darts,
But tonight, under these curtains of the dark,
We shall bask under a different kind of sunlight,
Hold my hand will you, let's watch the sun go down,
And until morning, I promise to not let you frown.
———————————————————————————————————————Downpourofwords

Footnote: *Some thoughts or poems hold their worth
in not being explained, but in being felt.*

Disparity in corners

One corner of the room said to the other,
What transpired here, did it even matter?
What was it all about, all that banter?
People making a mockery, in baking disaster,
For the air it still whispers in those voices,
The invisible ones, holding lives in vices,
With pangs made of a slimy something,
That slips but binds onto the inner skin,
The corner on the left was a cynical prick,
It captured all those incidents in a silent pic,
It piles them up, in files big and thick,
While the other corner in the courtroom, it just sits tight,
Watching the gravel comes down every so often,
And to try answer the questions that beckon.

—————————————————Downpourofwords

Footnote: *A poetic rendition of what goes on in a courtroom, and an analogy to one side of the room being smeared with all the incidents & the associated wrong, the pain, the hurt, the violence, the injustice being tried out, versus another side that sees, observes & contemplates the incidents with open eyes.*

Only northbound

What I can conjure up, out of thin air,
Must be something good, it's only fair,
For what didn't exist before & does now,
Will stand the test of time, the question is how.
And words have that power to forever hold on,
In rough tides, often cheering up faces forlorn,
Or to propel souls deep rooted in the ground,
Into the skies or at least drive them northbound,
Words are also like the feelings often felt,
That make our hearts kneel, & oftentimes melt,
Or to act like a shot in the arm for many,
Who maybe dealing with some form of adversity?
Guess the words reside in me for a reason
To be penning thoughts, free from any inhibitions.
——————————————Downpourofwords

Footnote: *I have often asked myself "why do I write?". More than anything, I find sanctity in an answer that means my words being a moment of comfort, a moment of joy, a moment of revelation, a moment of affection felt, a moment of contemplation, a moment of acceptance but more than anything, a moment of feeling better after reading.*

Knocking on life's door

Why do I do the things the way I do,
And why do I think the way I now do?
Is there a pattern in all this though?
Or do I keep watering my thoughts down a slope?
Is there a certain method to my madness?
Is there a reason behind my bouts of sadness?
For it's hard to try and chain to words,
All my blissful & unnerving emotions that come in hordes,
The frailties and negativity around included,
Alongside possibilities of life, waiting to be unloaded,
It's not the why that puts me in a spot,
But the how, it matters, & it matters a lot,
And then I find myself at a door that I stand I knock,
Waiting, holding a key, hoping that it just might work.
———————————————————Downpourofwords

Footnote: *We all have wants & asks from our lives. What are yours? What is that door that you stand in front of, with a key to opening up the possibilities that you await?*

In broad daylight

When you set your sights somewhere high,
There's not much time to heave and sigh,
For the time, it zips past at 150 something miles,
From exciting times to those candid smiles,
From confusing times to revelations rather stark,
From unexpected memories to twisted tales apart,
When you know you have a mountain to climb?
You can't fathom leaving your dreams, in a bind,
For they need to be unwrapped, albeit elegantly,
To be placed on a pedestal, & watered daily,
For only our actions are the green pill for our dreams,
Letting them prosper, bustle from the seams.
If what you seek to find is indeed unique,
There'll be an unmasking one fine day, in broad daylight.
—————————————————Downpourofwords

Footnote: *To be living & not be carrying dreams is a sham, to be wanting & not act upon is a sham. And to give up on hope without a try, is a sham. Life shall surpass us in a hurry if we let things be, & that's why pursuing one's dreams wholeheartedly becomes a necessity. And one day, there shall be a realization of those dreams, in broad daylight.*

Holding on

I saw that rope dancing in the waters,
Flickering at will, as it ran helter-skelter,
It did have a sparkling hook, to be tethered,
Holding on to it, was all that mattered,
But the rope was pulled on away,
Causing it to vigorously flip and sway,
Pulled by chains from the world so vane,
Driven by greed, insecurities & acts rather lame,
Lending me obstacles & life would never be the same.
And that's when I saw hope slightly giving away,
It was a moment of feeling frittered away.
In my mind, I was about to lose my way,
That's when I heard the cauldrons roar,
Egging me to uphold my inner uproar,
And I did, holding on with all that I had,
If you ask me now, hell yeah, I am glad.

——————————————Downpourofwords

Footnote: *At times along with the inhibitions that we carry in our minds, there are also acts or deeds from people that add on to the obstacles we face. Most times, such acts are driven by envy, insecurities or a simple way of trying to stall someone's journey to success. Do not lose heart & keep playing your rightful part, & if you do so enough times, there will be a day you will look back & feel proud of where you reach.*

Nipped in the bud

Dispelled into a web of notions by birth,
Starting low on a pedestal of human girth,
Self-belief, restrained in human chains,
Shackles unseen, dispensing immense pains,
Weird though, no scars are seen on the outside,
Rather prevailing as permanent blotches inside,
Dreams as subtle, as a new beginning,
Start to get brittle with time, unrelenting,
For what is a careless dream, as a young child;
Needs nurturing, to not be tossed around in violent winds,
Of caution, negation, nipping dreams in the bud,
Like putting down a horse that's was ready to stud,
Who does this though? It's the words "You Can't"
Said to little kids, when just making a start.

—————————————————Downpourofwords

Footnote: *The words "You can't" said to a child can have a profound impact on their psyche. It is of course necessary for things that are wrong, but never so for something that's possible, especially if it involves doing something right, something difficult. It is akin to nipping a child's dreams in the bud, increasing the number of things they grow up learning as not possible.*

Shower thoughts

A yawn escaped my lips as I walked,
And turned on the shower & momentarily basked,
A thought from last night, it haunted,
I wasn't writing enough, & I was frustrated.
A smirk escaped my faintly wetted lips,
As my mind conjured up a spark of light,
An idea about a poem nice and bright,
Creativity and showers, I wondered if they are tied?
A heartfelt smile, it escaped my conscience,
As I reveled in showers & thoughts about some poems,
In a desperation to write, I showered a lot,
My skin started to welt, started developing knots,
The showers went on, & then the thoughts stopped,
I wrote a poem as dream broke, and I woke up.

———————————————Downpourofwords

Footnote: *It is indeed true that showers can help with creativity. A poem about being flooded with creative thoughts during a shower, which actually turned out to be a dream, yet ended up with a poem being penned.*

Penny thoughts

How long ago was a pen invented?
And since when has it, been taken for granted,
For the masses & the literate world knows,
That a pen has been mightier than a sword.
It was a pen that long ago liberated,
Thoughts that bled onto a paper, unabated,
And that's when many a foundation were laid,
For literature to stand apart, in an enlightened shade,
But slowly though, the power from the mighty pen,
Started strife's even amidst the kith and kin,
Started being used more often like a weapon,
Piercing with words or rules unleashed from oblivion,
And here we stand today, passing on a baton
From a pen to our fingertips, while interesting times beckon!
————————————————Downpourofwords

Footnote: *Ever since the act of writing took birth, the purpose of writing has been applied to life in many ways. As creativity, as rules, as laws, as advice, and at times as a means to bring down an empire or a person as well. The act of writing will go on, even if a pen is now replaced by the dancing fingertips.*

Fire on my tail

I want to be that blazing airplane,
With a blazing fire on my tail,
I would then soar deep into those skies,
Looking behind, to see some faces in smiles,
Onboard will be people pre-screened,
A little fire in the belly to be seen,
To tear ahead into places never been,
Away from hurtful thoughts, best left unseen,
There shall be a bump, as we transcend,
Into a realm of possibilities unseen,
And as you bask in blissful aura and sheen,
On those clouds with carpets lush green,
I shall shut off the engine, dive down again,
As more await to get onboard my plane.

——————————————————————————-Downpourofwords

Footnote: *A wishful poem on wanting to be someone to make a positive difference in the lives of many, & to keep doing so time and again, onboard a whimsical plane.*

Albeit in smiles

When you are riding on the waves,
You need to know which way it sways,
For mysterious are the different ways,
That dreams take you on, as the heart sways.
Vicious thoughts, and hurtful doubts,
Pessimistic thoughts, in repeated bouts,
Weird are the questions that get asked,
Inside the mind, which is mostly packed,
But hang around for after that high tide,
Is a slope which you shall undoubtedly like,
For when on the slide, you hold the steely reigns,
That shall decide how far you get to throw your weight,
Up & over that next monstrous higher tide,
Sailing over the obstacles like there's no other time,
And some day, after conquering few high tides,
You shall be doing it all the time, albeit in smiles.

—————————————Downpourofwords

Footnote: *There will be doubts, there will be fears that we will continue to feel until the time we are alive. Mastering the art of living with them, accepting their presence as a part of our own, to then be comfortable riding them to reach where we want to be.*

Perfect host

The tears that she silently wept,
The nights that she barely slept,
Were from promises that she never kept,
Promises made long ago with intent,
Ones that with time, withered away in strength,
To the lure and the glitter of life, omnipresent,
Inside her mind though, the thoughts-constant,
Leading even to actions worthy of repent,
And in time, he started to see, to feel,
What was once, to now-what it had become.
She wept a few days and hopped on,
Onto the next subway train looking on,
For her next perfect host to devour on,
She had was a master in an Art of walking on.
————————————————Downpourofwords

Footnote: *Don't some live their lives switching hosts, knowing what it takes yet welcoming the unwanted ghosts?*

Dallas rains

On a certain stormy Sunday afternoon,
When the cell phones went off in unison,
And the clouds laid a carpet of the unknown,
The rain started to pour, with a vigor its own.
There was a haze from the water pouring, unfazed,
And the rain drenches the shrubs that as well, felt grazed,
But soon changed its mind, & veered to right,
And my eyes watched, being amazed by the sight.
And somewhere in that moment in time,
I started seeing a pattern, in the rain, sublime,
Of hazy human forms riding the winds, in a line,
No faces, no color, saw a human progression in sight,
And I wondered if someone else back in time,
Had watched these rains, to have felt alike,
The Dallas rains stopped just as quick as they came,
Left a fleeting thought, as I wondered if I was insane.
——————————————————Downpourofwords

Footnote: *Oftentimes the shapes we see in nature appear to be something else or leave behind a thought. One of such instances while watching an untimely downpour that seems to come out of nowhere & poured like there was no tomorrow.*

A little part

I will hope on till I can hope on,
Until the time I can straddle on,
Riding on a black unicorn in my mind,
Feeling the raging winds, one of a kind,
For I see a meaning in keeping on moving on,
Than to keep turning back, to those sad songs,
Like a frozen movie stream, with audio on,
Maybe there's good reason in marching on,
For I see there's a never-ending need,
That I could in some way tend to, feed,
And until there's a hope in that part,
I shall hang on to my words, with all I got,
For I have found a meaning in my Art,
And I know I am playing a little part.
——————————————Downpourofwords

Footnote: *In writing with a hope that these words will one day make a difference, is a blissful feeling of essence.*

A sky of Butterflies

I have a battle with words, & it never ends,
From ocean floors to mountain tops, & unseen bends,
It transcends into many an avenue, often bright,
And as well those darker depths, bereft of light,
The words they come & go at times, like a rainbow,
Every so often, encapsulating me in a halo,
But I have a game, in which I get to play catch,
Where butterflies named thoughts, they fly past,
And I have a hook made of chrome that I use,
To snatch them butterflies & paint a worldly muse,
At times my words feel weird and abused,
Other times staring back at me, with me amused,
I intend to fight on, I intend to write on,
A part of my sky with my butterflies is all I want
——————————————Downpourofwords

Footnote: *A imaginary rendition of looking upon every thought of mine that found its form as a poem being compared to a butterfly in the sky. By the time I am done, would I see a sky full of colorful butterflies?*

Give or take

The randomness of your care,
The suddenness of your despair,
The seldom'ness of your talks,
The awkwardness in your walks,
The abundance of your tantrums,
The existence of your hallucinations,
The prominence of your dominance,
The abstinence from your happiness,
The tepidness of your decisions,
The concussions from your confusions,
The emptiness of your confessions,
The waywardness is your conversations,
All these also make you who you are,
With not a lot to give or take, by and far.

—Downpourofwords

Footnote: *What makes some people hard to trust, to rely on? A lot of the above.*

Then, she walked

The stranger she saw in the dark,
Was a shadowy figure from her past,
Maybe not, but that's what she thought,
For she had a mind that slogged a lot,
Almost akin to a creaky finetuned rustic clock,
That never forgot it's persistent tick tock,
And persistence in her did eventually take stock,
Even with boulders laid in her path, not just rocks,
For the demons from her dark they stomped, not walked,
In broad daylight, at times when she would let them talk.
But once again like before, she pulled up on her socks,
Yanked the chains, ruffled up some rustic locks,
Saw the demon raise its ugly hood, higher on out,
And she hit back at it, with a hope filled club, so stout,
And this time she smiled more, as she walked,
One final time putting the demons of past, behind her back.

———————————————————Downpourofwords

Footnote: *There's a certain something in some women who do not give up, on anything. Despite being subjected to adversity, due to the society, they straddle on in the end, singing their hopeful songs.*

I race, tomorrow

Tomorrow is the day I shall race,
Once again, & this time with a newfound grace,
For the last time I was in a race,
Fear and me, had come face to face,
And I had stood tall till the end,
I was stubborn, not willing to bend,
And I shall climb, run, jump again,
Even feel those gentle, nimble pains,
But between all this, I shall have fun,
As I challenge myself, whilst on the run,
What started off as a test drive, is now a scenic drive,
The realizations that dawn at times, are worthwhile,
I shall do my best, to cross that finish line,
And to the essence of fitness, here's a hi-five.
————————————————Downpourofwords

Footnote: *A poem written on the night prior to participating in a Spartan Sprint race in 2019. Spartan race is an obstacle race which involves multiple physically challenging obstacles with a specific start & finish. An experimental participation became a routine of sorts and so can be the act of engaging in some form of fitness, if done with a steely resolve & dedication.*

Across the finish line

Woke up this morning, feeling quite ok,
Had a race to start and finish, then come back ok.
It started off well under the summer heat,
I could almost hear a passerby's heartbeat.
Lost my earphones right before the start,
Oopsie moment, there was no looking back,
Didn't have my upbeat songs as my company,
Yet had the presence of them Spartans aplenty,
Second time lesson learnt, hydrating well,
Right before a race is basic, & very crucial.
A few cramps midway meant I had to buckle up,
If I had to trod on until the victory lap,
Had known this time it would be more of mind over body,
I did it, added another medal to a kitty I call as my booty.

—————————————————Downpourofwords

Footnote: *A poem written after finishing the Spartan sprint race in June 2019. The hiccups shall always be there. It is more about how we gulp them down with intent, to be able to wade across that finish line. 5 Spartan medals & counting.*

If I could, you could too

I have loitered in those dark places often,
Where laziness engulfed me like a demon,
And I felt like a flagpole amidst a pile of rubble,
Feeling my presence, yet in a way nimble,
I have uprooted those wires and traveled far,
Many a times, yet fallen back off the radar,
And now I know fitness doesn't belong in a place far,
It's to be kept near, like a never-ending war.
And it feels like war only up to a certain point,
After which it sticks around with us, conjoined.
I ain't a fitness beast but I do eat my feast,
Of beautiful walks or runs, random reps, at least,
If you are loitering like a lost flagpole right now, worry not,
Take a first step and leave that drudgery alone, to rot.

—————————————Downpourofwords

Footnote: *Being fit is a dream for many. Being fit is an obsession for many. And being fit is a way of life for many. Yet in the walks of life, we often see more of the ones who want to engage in fitness yet fall short, time & again. Even the act of riding a bicycle was learnt after plenty a fall, but once a certain threshold of balance is acquired, it stays on for a lifetime. With fitness, the threshold must be crossed multiple times, until it becomes a prominent part of our lifestyle.*

Scary little things

The way of life, lived taking shortcuts,
Is filled with thrills, bruises as well as little cuts,
That appear one by one onto an unsuspecting a soul,
Hidden layers deep, inside a dark inner core,
They start like mold, in ways mildly scavenging,
And end up being rather enticing, & truly conniving,
For the lure of getting to a good place soon,
It sets into motion, a soul's unseen doom,
But for a tongue that has reveled in the taste of blood,
What's family, a vision or a bond or a brood?
It's like drifting down a lovely looking slope,
Not knowing where it takes you, where it really goes,
The ride seems fun just for the speed it brings,
Even if a ditch awaits down below, filled with scary little things.
——————————————Downpourofwords

Footnote: *In almost every twist & turn that life throws upon us, we are dealt with choices, even if it means choosing between two options filled with nothing more than discomfort or between two options that would fill us with love, abundance & other good things. Whilst being at a precipice of making a decision, it is not that hard to find a shortcut, a quick way to getting to a better place. And there's usually a price to be paid with every known shortcut. The extent to which people can go, to getting there faster is a sorry tale unfortunately. Compassion, consideration, empathy and the like get tossed out the window most times when taking shortcuts. But for what? And is there a real sense of fulfillment from having reached to a seemingly better-looking place through shortcuts?*

Victory over constant

If not here, where else would I be,
If not this, what else would I be?
If not now, when shall I turn the key,
If not me, who else is it gonna be?
Aren't these pertinent questions in reality?
Inkling thoughts in all of us, bereft of disparities.
If life is a well-known to-be-lived mystery,
Questions are the apostles upholding a victory,
A victory of change over the constant,
A victory of possibility over sedentary, imminent,
For without questions how would we even learn?
Be caught up in a mad rush to stockpile, to earn?
It's in the present though that all the answers lay,
To what our future protects, neatly tucked away.

——————————————————————Downpourofwords

Footnote: *Change we know, is the only constant. And to change for the better is a wish omnipresent. To be someplace else, to be like someone else, to be with someone else, to be something else, these thoughts shall & will remain as tender thoughts in most of us, even though the frequency of the same vary from person to person. Yet, the truth resides in being actionable, in changing things in the right way, in things that matter to us in a unique way.*

Blind recluses

The dry leaves on the ground tell a tale,
Laying crumpled, abandoned, looking pale,
Where once greenery resided amidst them chirps,
A bison now lurks leaving out dry, acidic burps.
Where once a shade of comfort resided,
Abandonment and loneliness hath now presided,
Where once three harmonious species lived, as a family,
Filling days and nights with sounds, & activity,
Is now seen a deathly silence that glares,
Glaring back at mankind with red bloodshot eyes,
For what mankind sought to gain in abundance,
Led to a demise of other peaceful existences,
And we excel in the Art of making excuses,
In seeing just fine yet finding blind recluses.
————————————————Downpourofwords

Footnote: *As we humankind has rolled on over generations, we have been blind more often than not to certain species vanishing into pages of history, to be remembered as pictures & descriptions than in real life. And we continue to do so by being spectators to be a reason for wiping out different life forms in the remote mountains or in the depths of the oceans far from where we live. The poem is about the act of being comfortable with the fact as long as human life moves on comfortably.*

When mirror flew

She named him a parrot,
For he spoke too sweet,
He named her a sparrow,
For she sang so mellow,
He fixed her a nest,
High up in the mountains,
She showed him a mirror,
A little one, his other future,
He made friends with foes,
To live in peace, not chaos,
She pointed the mirror to the sky,
Said that's where your future lies,
Fly all you can but also try,
To send a bird or two more into the sky,
And mirror, it flashed really bright,
Started his ascent to the skies.

—————————————Downpourofwords

Footnote: *A poem about a bird that a couple brought & fell in love with, called it a parrot, a sparrow & then named it a mirror for it reflected more of love & what they liked to see, & even in its flight, it left behind a lesson or two.*

Diabetic Love

She worked at the bakery in the corner,
Monday to Friday from eight to four,
She could beat the clock if she ever wished,
That's what people said, & they called her Ms. Nice,
It wasn't at the bakery that Mr. Brat,
He named himself that, he first saw her at a park,
She held a baby sheep like her own little part,
And that's when he first felt a tiny spark,
Wasn't into sweets, but was a moment sweet,
He became a clock all around the week,
He brought a pastry then on, every single day,
A word or two more exchanged in any little way,
And as their love story started to flourish,
A homeless man got admitted as diabetic.

—————————————————Downpourofwords

Footnote: *A fleeting love story which started as love at first sight &
blossomed there on into something beautiful & left a hungry homeless
man diabetic in its wake, from being given all the pastries & the cakes.*

Not counting miles

These moments of my life that flip by,
With me resembling a stranger, looking by,
Being amazed as the things they transpire,
Wondering if this is what I had once aspired,
Worrying if I am ahead or far off behind,
In a jigsaw puzzle residing in my own mind
For in the maze out there, lies a game,
Addictive like crushing candies, even if lame.
I used to once play that stupid game,
Hell, I even dreamt of a hall of fame,
But then it struck me like a lightning,
There a calm in acting right, in just being,
And then I see the puzzle turn into a straight line,
And I walk along smiling, not counting my miles.

—Downpourofwords

Footnote: If you continue to do things that feel right, there's not much to worry, even when the destination isn't quite in sight. The essence of engaging in doing right things and in devoting time to things that matter is in itself sufficient at times to wade through questionable times.

For you, I shall pray

All the things you tell me I can't do,
Do you yourself believe it to be true?
For you can reign me on the outside,
But not the seas that thrive in me deep inside.
They have the strength to even move boulders,
To even carry others along, on able shoulders,
You for sure have control on some of my actions,
But none in my inner realm of imaginations.
How will you tame the silent waters?
Or my raging waves that keep creating flutters?
What's in me is very much a part of me,
What I do inside is my sacred place to be.
The next time you use the word 'Don't',
Look within and ask if you really should,
We are who we are and what we say,
That's all for now, but for you I shall certainly Pray!
————————————————————————Downpourofwords

Footnote: *At times we run into people in our lives, people who are more into what occurs or transpires in another's life, than in their own. And it becomes all but obvious that there's a certain something they derive out of being so involved, so concerned with things they can influence in your life, that they lose track of where they themselves are headed. The poem intends to dwell into the thought that there's only so much that external factors can affect someone, so long as there is a belief in one's own abilities & on the way forward.*

Selfless Duty

What is it like to be a cop's wife?
Or for that matter a policeman's child,
For every morning there's a see you later,
Which could make the heart to quiver and shiver,
A parting hug is also packed with a prayer,
For going to work is in a way laced with danger.
Being a cop, to walk out & not to predict a day,
For events the unfold don't listen, they just say,
And to still wear a smile in the evening,
Even after seeing a farce or violence, or an act demeaning,
It takes much more than an emboldened mind,
To be engaged in a service of that kind.
What is it like to spend an entire day?
And not be engulfed in worry, to make peace in a way,
Make peace with uncertainty, with a refill of everyday pride,
To be walking alongside one in service, a humanitarian ride.
The family of the ones in duty each have a story,
Of loved ones who are known, more often for bravery,
And also, a story of how well they themselves cope,
In living a content life, driven by pride, refueled by hope.

—————————————Downpourofwords

Footnote: *To sign up for a service as a Cop, a policeman, someone in security or even the army, navy or the air force, it takes a decision of gumption. Along with praise & respect for the ones who sign up for such a job, there needs to be respect for the family of the ones in service too. An artist paints the tree more often than he paints the shadow, but do we ever wonder what would happen if the shade we seek under a tree ceases to exist?*

Purpose

What should your most vivid dreams be?
Standing atop Olympus mons on Mars?
Or to reach a pedestal so you could wipe some scars?
What should your work ethic rather be?
Like an industrious, visionary buzzing bee?
Or a lazy half floating, half walking Manatee?
What shall true happiness mean to thee?
Half a ladder from Maslow's hierarchy,
Or a life lived nodding to an anarchy?
What shall your true inner fears be?
To live an abundant life collecting things,
Or to live a life that's filled with memories?
What should your soul's inner quest be?
To feel, experience & grow internally,
Or leaving behind a world, as a better place to be?
—————————————————Downpourofwords

Footnote: *A life lived without a purpose, is an unending barrage of thoughts with "I Suppose". Why is it that we do things the way we do? What is it that drives us to wake up every morning? What is it that we intend to change by the time we are done? What is it that we crave to wish to learn from life? Purpose in life is as necessary as the air we breathe.*

Be watchful, of people

Don't lean too far on ahead,
For you might have a fall instead,
If the people you blindly rely on,
Don't fathom the essence of your kind.
Don't dwell too deep either,
For you might tremble and shiver,
If you let those expectations build,
Most of the world follows a flashy guild.
Don't jump too high up above in hope,
For people who envy you, don't know to cope,
Shall carry scissors to severe your high-flying ropes,
And then rejoice with empty-some souls.
Don't get too caught up in their lies,
Nor in the lies your mind bakes, it does try,
For lies at times seem to bring about a peace,
Conniving & lure-filled, giving a false air of ease.

———————————————Downpourofwords

Footnote: *The world we live in is advanced, in every which way. The words spoken at face value unfortunately need t be weighed in, probed in most cases to be able to believe. The acts that people can put up to make you believe, are in hindsight acts meant to deceive. And you shall be left in a bad spot if your decisions aren't made from a state of peace. Listen rather well, Contemplate & dwell, choose what to believe, Act more on your instincts.*

The perfumes you wear

What essence of yours will I feel,
When I am close to you, on an even keel?
Will it be a scent, soothing & light?
Like the one you wear often, when we dine?
Or will it be the other scent, bold and strong?
That depicts you, boldly righting them wrongs,
Will it be a scent that soothes me from inside?
Sending a wave of calm, relaxing my mind?
Or will it be the scent that draws me to you,
Making me get closer & closer to you?
Will it be a scent that gives me the hope?
To feel alive, to hang on to your rope.
What shall it be, tell me if you will,
You are the reason I feel like going for the kill,
Your presence in itself is a sacred gift,
Without you I would have long gone adrift.

—————————————————Downpourofwords

Footnote: *A heartfelt rendition of a presence to be grateful for, expressed using my addiction to perfumes/scents.*

The eyes that talk

The way your eyes playfully talk,
At times makes me stumble in my walk,
And as well causes a flutter in my heart,
Tickling my untouched mind part by part.
The way your eyes playfully stalk,
Makes me conscious, from being watched,
And as well instills a comfort of its own,
From a feeling of essence, of being known.
The way your eyes hit their mark,
Striking a chord right within my heart,
Leaving within me, a trail full of hope,
Lending me the strength to march, to cope.
The way your eyes make me talk,
Unraveling the innermost of my thoughts,
They say a lot without saying a lot,
It's in silence that words mean their most.

—————————————————Downpourofwords

Footnote: *Often times, words fall short of what the eyes end up conveying while other times even the choicest of words leave behind doubts, from not believing.*

Lost in a crowd

Walking in a crowd, I sometimes see me slide,
See myself lifting off the ground, drifting to the side,
And the wind beneath my feet, I feel at peace,
Even amidst banter & little children's screams.
The noises in my head they miraculously disappear,
Soon enough I see beautiful landscapes appear,
Of places where the wind whistles, blows calmly,
And the sun shines on well fed clouds that look heavenly.
These moments of being lost, while in a crowd,
Are seldom yet resonate with my side that's wild as well as loud,
Such moments, they leave me with a fleeting thought,
That the mind is also a lovely place to be lost.
I drift back again into reality in a while,
Having replaced a developing frown, with a smile,
Life at times is nothing but a beautiful chance,
To pick on mundane moments & to make them dance.
——————————————Downpourofwords

Footnote: *The biggest gift that the humankind has received is the gift of imagination. It is through imagination that we have come so far from the days of wandering in the jungles. And yet as we seem gnawed at from every side today by technology, the gift of imagination isn't drawn from as much as it should be. And there lies our biggest fallacy.*

One fine day?

Will there be a change one fine day?
When all the worries shall be cast away,
For us to live our days, not to just live another day,
When words spoken have more of truth, to convey.
When there's a lot more of hope & much else to beg, to pray.
Will there be a change one fine day?
When more smiles are seen on every face,
And hunger is a choice exercised, & not a way,
When the whole world accepts as us, people transsexual & gay,
When Compassion fills the air in almost every way.

There's purity Black and White, no in the shades of grey,
Would colors of the skin vanish one fine day?
Would life seem simpler in every given way,
Where words spoken are true, from hearts wanting to say?

How beautiful would the world then be, in being that way,
When sharing is caring, & lives are no more wasted away,
If perfection is what humankind seeks, in most ways,
Why then does a communion of happiness, seem so far away?
———————————————Downpourofwords

Footnote: *A poet's wishful wanting of a future world where there's more happiness than there is darkness, where there's more mutual respect than treacherous paths to be tread, where there's more meaning to the beauty of life & life itself, where there more beauty in ours hearts & more awareness about ourselves.*

Were you with me all this while?

If you were with me all this while,
Why did my face not adorn a smile?
Did you forget the moments that you made me cry?
To let me see days when my tear glands go high and dry?

If you were with me all this while,
Why then, did you wear that wicked guile?
And left me stranded in a place far away,
To be lost in a maze, in trying to find my way.

If you were with me all this while,
Why did you have those mean words to say?
And using ignorance to hurt me. in many ways,
To leave me in the dark, searching for rays.

If you were with me all this while,
Why then, did I have to walk those lonely miles?
There's a way to be together even when far,
There's a more subtle way to one's heart, without leaving a scar.

—————————————————Downpourofwords

Footnote: *An often repeated & acknowledged mistake in life is to take people for granted, even if they feature in our priorities as one's badly wanted. At what point does the distance become irreparable, it varies from person to person, but the truth though is that some walk away to never return, once they have departed.*

Distant together

We sit apart now, a thousand miles,
Yet I can feel your faint little smile,
And I can hear your thoughts, just as they flow,
Right by my ears, as a gush of wind, it gently blows.
I can feel you in my thoughts,
It's weird this feeling, I sense these growing knots,
Whoever thought even weirdness can be fun,
Your thoughts, they keep my heart firing like a misfiring gun.
I guess once in a while when I solemnly think,
Of you, you do as well maybe, as I feel a heartfelt blink.
In unison, in a moment bereft of any science,
Being engulfed by an ambience, bereft of signs.
I wonder if these thoughts could ever carry,
You to me or me to you, ever so gently,
We could spend an hour together, not in thoughts,
Looking into one other, being lost in talks.

—————————————————Downpourofwords

Footnote: *If everything we felt had an explanation, wouldn't our lives be more like a dreary mime, without any exclamations? To feel is a gift, to drift in the essence of a feeling is also a gift. To then feeling a feeling in unison is an ethereal bliss.*

Your thoughts galore

Into the clouds is where I sometimes drift,
Carried by winds made from your thoughts that I sift,
I feel lighter at times than ever before,
Sailing into the winds, carried by your thoughts galore,
It is when I soar into the skies, that I notice,
A flutter I feel deep inside, one with an essence of ease,
If mere these thoughts can be so powerful,
Being together I wonder would be purely blissful,
The clouds I sail amidst, are made of a faintly pink,
With sparkling rays at tandem, forcing me to blink,
I look around and I see you elegantly perched,
Resembling a hypnotic damsel, on a grandiose feathery raft.
I hold onto my thoughts to get closer to you,
And almost faint seeing that absolute beauty of you,
I sense my time freezing, right when our eyes meet,
I sense my otherwise fit mind, shudder a little, going weak.

——————————————————Downpourofwords

Footnote: *What is beauty if unappreciated, what are feelings if not reverberated? What is praise if its not heartfelt, what are moments if left unappreciated?*

A clingy friend

The pain that resides deep inside,
Perched in some people, at times is meant to hide,
For even its presence out in the open,
Could easily cause many a spirit to dampen,
For its darkness that is like a deadly lullaby,
Lures the others into ugly pangs, filled with misery.

Some forces of nature are left best hidden,
Some roads in life are best not taken.
I wonder at times if pain is a clingy friend,
Or a master in the act of disguise, or that of pretense,
For even when it lives inside, it does a vanishing act,
Making me wonder if it's a myth or a fact.
I think pain loves going on out, on scavenging walks,
Away from those souls, even if for a while, into the dark,
To let them shine in a moment of light, to feel a spark,
To try once again, to let those hearts into a park,
Where happiness & joy welcome them in open arms,
Even if the feeling feels stark & out of the norm,
I send a prayer to those hurting in pain,
I wish for pain to take frequent walks out of them, when it rains.

—————————————Downpourofwords

Footnote: *Pain is inevitable they say. Is there a way out of it, in any which way? Or is the way in acknowledging its presence as we wade through our days? If anything, we can be tactful in luring pain out of our way, even if for a while to send it packing away. There are some who hurt more than the ones who crave for pain, there are some who look at pain as a way to make gains. I pray for the ones who hurt in genuine ways & find cover in the rains.*

A warm fuzzy huddle

On a bartered raft, as I sailed along,
Badly wanting my radio to play a song,
When days felt dreary, & nights too long,
Losing sight of my present, even the right or wrong.

I drifted into the deep blue, feeling utterly lost,
With a heart made of stone, yet smitten by frost,
From coldness of the people around, and the past,
From acts of deceit, that are widely & sadly a part,
Of the world we live in where narcissistic tendencies,
Have made a home in people filled with dependencies.

I see a mountain range ahead, & a distant fire,
Fire from the presence of a demon named desire,
Ignited by the sinister people, dancing on a livewire,
A herd that dances along, basking n their acts so dire,
It's a lure that can get to many a minds',
But not ones like me, who believe in being kind,
I hold on my sail, steer it against them tides,
A little further, & I see those wicked smiles,
I make a turn and begin to use a measly paddle,
And soon enough I am embraced by kindness, in a warm & fuzzy huddle.

—————————————————Downpourofwords

Footnote: *Everyone in today's world is a hypocrite, but there are levels. Everyone in today's world is a narcissist, but there are levels. There is also strength in acknowledging the facts & more so in being aware of oneself, & one's own acts. The people who act mean every so often, are ones who have skipped a lecture or two on kindness & those on compassion.*

Mr. Mundane

They wished good night every night with a kiss,
On a dream run they were, very little else to really miss,
Their days were bright & the nights were warm,
Dawns till realms of dreams, the smiles were a norm,
They made new friends, & also got into groups,
It didn't take long to filter good ones from the crooks,
They were too lost in each other to even notice,
That life had other plans for them, ones filled with malice,
And there's only so much two hearts can find solace in company,
Of others that is, when two hearts beat in a symphony.
It sent along a demon, rightly named it Mr. Mundane,
Stealthily it could drive the wisest of minds insane,
They were in Love but were also mere mortals,
Started to wobble from unforeseen tantrums.
Started by pointing fingers, grew into baseless accusations,
Their plentiful silent moments, led to growing confusions,
Aided by their lack of actions, as well a lack of imagination,
Led to the downfall of a blossoming, love filled relation.

—————————————————Downpourofwords

Footnote: *The act of socializing if often overstretched in today's relationships. Socializing in many ways has become a means to fill the void that exists & grows between two adults. It can act in weird ways, encapsulating a couple to be drawn into endlessly socializing, instead of trying to fight Mr. Mundane head on. And before they know, life goes on & goes long, until there's a playlist that plays, filled with sad songs.*

Her deadly kiss

She said sure with a smile,
A smile that transcended miles,
She had this eerie, unnerving presence,
A storm he saw in her, beneath her sweet silence.
Even an affirmation seemingly harmless & gentle,
Has at times, immense girth to dismantle,
A perfect heart, to then toss it out as splinters,
To writhe in pain, in spring, monsoon & cold winters.
He noticed, smiled & hopped hastily onto an outgoing train,
Away from her vice, & that impending pain,
Being wise in life, isn't just by reading books,
It is as well in seeing beneath those looks,
For if every assuring smile in life were to be true,
Why else would people venture out looking for the new?
He bid her guile a goodbye with a flying kiss,
He knew better to not be lured by her deadly kiss.
——Downpourofwords

Footnote: *At times even the most beautiful of a face & the most glistening of eyes can hide a web of wickedness hard to notice.*

Rewritten history

If it was only up to me,
I would build a dynasty,
One full of wisdom and mystery,
With a touché of whimsical fantasy,
Where lives would mildly fall apart,
Only to eventually join back, stronger in fact,
In a synergy driven more by positivity,
Bereft of any sense of humane captivity,
Where joy would be found often, in achieving,
And belief as existent as the act of breathing,
Where dreams could grow, to be monstrous,
In absence of curtailing negativity, so poisonous.
I know it's not really up to me,
But together there's still a possibility,
Of working towards a better formed society,
Where abundance is all places, & abundant are opportunities,
And in possibility there's always a mystery,
If unraveled in the right ways, can be rewritten, history.

————————————————————Downpourofwords

Footnote: *Can we call the society we live in as a place of equal opportunities? There is a certainly a framework available for anyone to create opportunities but if we believe these are equally available to one and all, we are living in a comforting bubble. Brilliance is often met with silence, ridicule or at time unacknowledged & to let this happen in silence is also an apathy. How can there be a society where abilities, talents & the inner hunger of a person to succeed are the pedestals on which a successful life can be envisioned?*

A heart like jelly

The silence between us, it doesn't belong,
In our sweet melody, in our love song,
It's very clear though that something is off,
As even a moment of silence it seems so long,
Like a demon waiting to devour an unsuspecting soul,
Silence, it engulfs our vibes, consuming our whole,
And to leave behind gaping holes-unknown,
For us to search a way out, on our own.
Unsuspecting my heart is, to this hollow,
An ocean of feelings inside, yet to feel shallow,
The moments I spend thinking what did transpire,
Can instead be spent in being inspired,
By life, by nature and all good things alike,
Instead of dealing alone with all this strife.
And then a frivolous thought it crosses my mind,
Taking me back to where I started, behind,
A word from you and a few words from me,
I wonder if we could dispel the wicked silence into the seas.

—————————————————Downpourofwords

Footnote: *At times, the heart acts more mellow than a jelly, to be going to & fro like an anomaly. To be feeling one moment that its now all over, to then be drifting in thoughts of wanting to start over, the tumultuous feelings of the heart are hard to forego.*

Good memories of you

You asked me if we have a faint chance,
To be like before, of getting back,
But do you notice my back, and the sack,
Filled with lies from you, lying flat,
Its weight cranes my neck in directions unknown,
Leaving behind a stifling yet numbing pain, my own,
But I have already set out on a jaywalk,
To rid the weight off my back, in the dark.
You ask me if I can ever forgive,
But do you realize all I did, was to give,
Without caring a lot but still caring a lot,
For things that mattered, things you conveniently forgot.
I would rather carry the weight of my dreams,
Then in dragging your silence or hate-filled screams,
I have no hate left, only good wishes for you,
All I carry now is the good memories of you.
—————————————————Downpourofwords

Footnote: *A breakup poem intending to convey
a goodbye, with good wishes alongside.*

A Vacation Some Place

I want to go to a place somewhere far,
Where there are no doors left ajar,
For those worries to come creeping inside,
With tentacles-sticky, long, slowing my slide,
For if a worry travels with me there,
The solace in me would run amok without a care.
My thoughts would then just be alive,
Like a thousand bees without honey and a hive.
Anxiety is ok, I see it as a necessary alibi,
It keeps my toes grounded, & my hopes high,
But I hate to see the worries hanging around,
More so when on a vacation, short or long.
I want an extra lock on such a door,
To keep away them worries, bitter and sour.

———————————————————————Downpourofwords

Footnote: *To be on a vacation & to be caught up in worries of the usual kind, is like watching your favorite movie with a hundred things to do on your mind. The essence of a vacation is not to click pictures or to count them likes but more to detach oneself from the daily life, to be able to revitalize one's zeal to deal with life in a better way.*

A life full of Saturday's?

What if all the Saturdays of our life,
Were to be brought together, to be in a line,
To then live a few years filled with Saturdays,
One after another, like spinning blades?
Ever wonder how that would really feel?
A dream come true, something too good to be real,
Or a knot in the gut from a hypnotic wheel,
Or a life filled with hope, a newfound zeal,
Would you skip a breakfast, brunch or a meal?
To do things differently, to feel how it feels?
What would we wait for then, day in-day out,
Would humanity be the same or an altogether different Gould?
I tried to change a calendar, it didn't work,
I turned to my mind, it listens, isn't such a dork.

—Downpourofwords

Footnote: *The craving for a weekend is an universal feeling of sorts. TGIF is an acronym known by more than 60% of the world's population. What would happen if humanity was let to live a few years filled with Saturday's on a calendar? How would we adopt? And what would happen to a necessity Called purpose in life?*

Not very far

I can feel the fleeting wind in the air,
There's something happening out there,
There's a calm breeze it carries a scent,
Of a feeling of feeling good in the present,
The wind I feel is one that blows with hope
It has honey traps set to gather the nopes,
I can sense a wave of action rising from above,
Pushing aside petty differences that have us on hold,
The wave though, also carries a blanket along,
With holes to let through showers of hope,
The blanket though has two of its ends caught,
Held down by those minds caught up in knots,
Or the ones hungry to just reserve their spots,
In being blind to possibilities of life, that indeed are a lot,
The winds are stronger now than before,
I sense an oncoming shade, not very far.
——————————————————Downpourofwords

Footnote: *A hopeful poem about a possible change in the world we live in. A change where the winds that blow around being about an aura of hope that engulfs the masses to move together as one, to confront our battles & obstacles as one, to feel a shade filled with calm like none other, whilst there will always be some who continue to hang on to things that do not matter.*

Opposite of yesterday?

Why is yesterday's opposite-tomorrow?
Shouldn't it ethereally be, the NOW?
For yesterday is about what once was,
And today is all about what there is,
And if in contemplation of a foregone yesterday,
Our sights get locked on the yet unseen day,
I wonder what happens to 'A new day', which is today,
Looks like it will be deftly tucked away.
Isn't it better to see a blur, than be totally blind?
It's a need, the future ought to be on the mind,
But why to crush today, in tomorrow's hindsight?
Once in a while, isn't it ok to take it a little light?
Aa another yesterday is bygone, as another tomorrow beckons,
What do we do today, can we all ponder, & reckon?
—————————————————————Downpourofwords

Footnote: *Between a yesterday, today & a tomorrow does get lived most of our lives. Yet there would be many a present day that we let go buried under the weight of either a yesterday or a tomorrow. To be aware & to learn from one's past is a need. To have a plan & vision for a future is a need. But to crush our todays for the past & the future, isn't that wise indeed.*

What would you rather be?

What would you rather be?
Be a reason for someone's envy,
Or be a victim of your own envy?
Be a reason for someone's misery?
Or a means to wipe off another's misery?
Be a reason for someone's happiness,
Or be on an unending quest for happiness?
Be a reason for someone's loneliness,
Or a means to ward off some loneliness?
Be a reason for someone's expectations,
Or be caught up in your own ocean of expectations?
Be a reason for someone's disappointment?
Or a person immune to disappointments?
Be a reason for someone's achievements,
Or a garden filled with meaningful achievements?
—————————————Downpourofwords

Footnote: *Purpose in life is an often-undervalued parameter & it is not so from the lack of intent, but from the lack of acceptance, existence of silence or ridicule from others, that seem omnipresent. Yet the way we perceive ourselves as playing a part in life makes a world of difference in what we do & where we end up being, in this journey called life.*

Where's your selfie?

Will there ever be such a selfie?
Which will not just grab a picture,
But also act as a door to enter,
The insides of our own characters?
What would the image look like?
A beautiful scenic view unique,
Or a canvas full of beaming smiles & mystique?
Or a frozen frame of confusing memes,
A picture meaningful yet stark?
Or a poster faded, painful and dark,
Would the selfie say a lot about you?
Or still hide what you really want to?
What story would the selfie depict,
One of hope or a downward slide?
It pays to sometimes look inside,
Selfie or not, self-reflection is an Art, meaningful to glide.

—————————————————————Downpourofwords

Footnote: *How many selfie's does your phone have? Probably a lot if you are someone who appreciates the way you were made. Is there a selfie that depicts you for who you really are, internally? The poem focuses more on the act of self-reflection, & the act of contemplation about oneself, about who we are, outside of the nuances of how we look, focusing more on how we feel, who we think we are.*

Love lingers

The days that I don't think about you,
They exist but count to a paltry few,
Most days you do cross my mind,
For our memories painted in gold solemnly reside,
In a place within me that's hard to hide,
And I acknowledge it to be a part of my ride.
I don't think you left me out in the cold,
Maybe we were meant to drift for the good,
The thoughts about you they do feel real,
And I wonder if I have feelings left to feel.
As I drift in these thoughts, I see your gentle smile,
Flashing like a beacon in front of my eyes,
And I lose my train of thought, like a little kid,
Excited about his first amusement park skid.
The days that I don't think about you,
Are the ones when I have a lot to do,
Someone has said and said it very true,
Love lingers, & is a feeling so very different, so very new.
———————————————————————Downpourofwords

Footnote: *A poetic rendition of Love and how it envisions
in many of us in different ways, often aided by memories or
moments from the past or moments that we lived openly without
hearts. To deny is a choice but to acknowledge can be a vice yet
doesn't the tumultuous feeling of love feel rather nice?*

Small-town dreams

Living in a suburb on a street unknown,
Dreaming of a mansion in LA downtown,
With a few sports cars parked up front,
From success from one's own abilities, yet not be adamant,
Living the life of a small-town cool guy,
Wanting to be a reason for other's envy & some joy,
Wearing clothes that could raise a few eyebrows,
Driving golf carts on them lush green meadows,
Living in a dreamy world created on his own,
With a raging hunger, of wanting to be known,
To then opening eyes to reality, slipping out a groan,
A fulfilling small-town life, & its essence unknown,
Living life blinded by the city life & the lure of gold,
Of people who have it all, have both feet up in the air,
From earning in millions in a life that seems so fair,
Perception though can plunge us into a deadly lair,
If blindly following things that we don't solemnly care,
Acknowledging what we have is also an unseen gift,
For if not, wayward dreams can take life adrift.

—— —Downpourofwords

Footnote: *Human life as it has evolved over the centuries has always been shaped by what we call as a herd mentality. If something works wonders for one person or a set of people, it doesn't take long for that to become the new norm. And as life has advanced with technology, the awareness is omnipresent which makes it easier to get drawn into believing that the lives of a select few are apostles that everyone should dream for. The poem depicts a small-town boy & his fascination with a abundant money filled life in LA, while living in a town filled with values of co-existence, proximity to nature & the bliss called simplicity of life.*

Moments, intense

As the door opened, her footsteps slowed,
Something in her inner core, it viciously moved,
A feeling in her heart it grew in size,
For a moment she stood, frozen in time,
She raced down the stairs and her heartfelt glare,
Met his, & a few silent moments blissfully flared,
Awakened by his footsteps & his presence,
And a hunger inside her raged, wild & intense,
To be in his embrace, to feel a gentle kiss,
Passionate as always, aching to relive that bliss,
Which often came from being so lost in one another,
That they floated into space in a different world altogether,
By being numb to every damn thing on the outside,
Being exposed to feelings felt deep inside,
All it took was a warm gentle hug to begin with,
For kisses to fill the silent air, to be ethereally drawn in,
Time froze into beautiful moments, a few times that night,
Feeling whole again, she hugged him & slept tight.
—————————————————Downpourofwords

Footnote: *To be born as a human & to not feel is unreal.*
A poem describing carefree moments of passion between two
who had an intense affection for one another's presence.

That dark spot

There's a dark spot on an empty wall,
It's protrudes but is minuscule and small,
It's holding on barely, looks ready for a fall,
Weighed down I think, by the thoughts about that wall,
Tiny in essence but it has a vivid presence,
Stays very still but takes me to places. In silence,
It draws my eyes & my mind into an enticing lullaby,
Frozen I am, in bed with thoughts awake, amicably,
It takes me to places I have never seen before,
Sliding into spaces, seemingly sweet as well as sour,
At times I feel trapped by that little dark spot,
In a circle of thoughts that just won't buzz off.
At times I feel a calm, in being bodily numb,
To everything outside & let my thoughts hop on & jump,
My eyes flicker, moving away from the spot,
And I look around, to then stare at the clock.

—————————————————Downpourofwords

Footnote: *A moment of staring at a dark spot on a wall that confined me physically but not mentally & how a moment of acknowledging its presence turned into a ride alongside my imaginative mind that knows no boundaries, to be lost in thoughts for a while.*

That unlived life

Has anyone ever lived a life,
Bereft of any worries or the worldly strife?
A life lacking any apprehensions of any kind,
Spent mostly in beautiful revelations of the mind?
Doesn't everyone have their share of moments,
Of anxiety, stress, impending decisions, & things to lament?
To then be compounded by sticky action items,
Of consequences & repercussions in life & its fulcrum.
Has anyone ever lived a life,
Where every decision made was first time right?
With most days spent feeling alright,
Never having to use actions or words as a sword or a knife?
Has anyone ever lived a life,
Where every person they met was perfectly in line,
With what they sought & was unbelievable kind,
To leave an essence unlike any other, in spreading smiles.
I wonder if the answer to all of these would be a yes,
For life is a paradox where even perfection is from a guess.
——————————————————Downpourofwords

Footnote: *Perfection is a myth they say & so is a perfect life. And to be alive comes along with the good & the bad, as moments that have to be had, in a journey where we see, feel, experience & we learn and move ahead constantly. To wish for our life to be free of worries is wishful thinking however it is truly up to us to keep life marching towards where we want it to be, one fine day.*

Lessons from ancient minds

Somewhere out there in the wild,
There is a battle that rages, as one of its kind,
A Battle Royale of survival of the self,
With survival as the only known form of stress.
A stress that transforms beautifully,
Into evolution of life forms in nonchalantly,
To change within and on the outside,
It's sure is one roughly ridden ride.
For in not adapting to the changing demands of survival,
Means a certain end to life, albeit any denials.
Like magic, the changes in life forms do occur,
Driven by need, and sometimes by fear,
And to accept the stress to survive is an act intrinsic,
To many a species that come & go, with life as their picnic,
And we humans with intellect have so many forms of stress,
Even in things means to be part of our experience,
Does it make sense for us to switch back in time?
To go back a little and read some ancient minds,
For learnings can be precious, from their lifetimes,
To be those answers we always want to find.

—————————————————Downpourofwords

Footnote: *Do we remember conversations from our grandfathers or great grandfathers about stress, mental disorders or the like? Chances are that such conversations would be by and far. And these are generations that lived through the great depression, world war I and II and through major catastrophic events as well. Why is it that we see a sudden spike in issues related to mental health? There must be something they did right in the way they lived & perceived life as which is different from the ways we deal with life today. Lessons are not always in the future.*

Most things

Most stories that unravel this real world,
Have seeds sown in the mind, to then unfold,
To then be transformed by life & its winds,
To be remembered as memories, with inklings.

Most places that reside in people's hearts,
Are colder from being repeatedly exposed,
To pain, deceit & hurt from the ones bold,
Bold in bending rules, ignoring the thresholds.

Most spoken words in this world,
Are wrapped neatly to look like gold,
Hiding most of what's truly inside,
In layers of deceit that elegantly hides.

Most fulfilling lives in the world, the one apart,
Are from carefree adventures of the heart,
In dreaming about something beautiful,
And chasing dreams until they are fruitful.
————————————Downpourofwords

Footnote: *It is not always what it seems as there is always something hiding beneath the seams.*

Where life thrives

A sky full of beautiful stars,
Isn't that all we dream for,
Or do we yearn for more?
To nourish our inner core.
A heart full of lucid dreams,
Of beautiful experiences yet unseen,
Friends-tall, short, thick or lean,
Loyal, fun and sometimes mean.
Or a Life filled with Love,
From everyone willing to give,
A job that pays our bills,
Yet keeps giving us the thrills.
Or a home filled with abundant peace,
Where happiness is for keeps.
In between us and the vastly skies,
Is a space where life, it thrives.

———————————————Downpourofwords

Footnote: *What is it that we all wish for? For wishes as well define the kind of life we live in between what life offers to us as experiences.*

The numbered chairs

Put a Democrat on chair number 1,
A humanitarian on chair number 2,
A well-known athlete on chair number 3,
A hardcore capitalist on chair number 4,
A visionary patented madman on chair # 5,
An honorary literary scholar on chair # 6,
Far from democrat, add a republican chair # 7,
An e-commerce magician on chair # 8,
A chivalric senior army man on chair # 9,
A yogic monk or a fitness freak on chair # 10,
A security wiz-kid with a laptop on chair#11
A Nobel laureate or a teacher on chair#12
Let the room be locked for a few hours of discussions,
After giving an agenda of worldly good & actionable actions,
To enable an idea fest of sorts to evolve from the meeting,
To set right a few things, like a new beginning.
————————————————————Downpourofwords

Footnote: *Often times we see that most people who make it to those apostles of power belong to a certain type even though there are exceptions. How to we make decision making that influences the world more inclusive? A poem tinkering this thought of a varied set of individuals who have proven their worth in their fields of excellence & have learned many a lesson through their determination, passion & in overcoming many a obstacle. What would the outcome be from such a conglomerate if an agenda is set forth clearly?*

And that bread

The number of books we buy, to not read,
But with just a wish, a need to be well read,
Would they serve a better purpose elsewhere?
For if it's about a balance, it seems just fair,
Either the books be read fair & square,
Or be handed over to another's lair,
For the words that keep bouncing in there,
Could find a better, more acceptant abode elsewhere,
In a place where a hungry mind awaits,
Wanting to learn, wanting to hone their traits,
But being caught up in life & in trying to earn that bread,
The books do collect dust causing a reason for dread,
Life's unfair in many ways as some minds with a want,
Don't have the moolah to buy books, they just can't,
Whilst at another place there's a pile of wonderful books,
Sitting unappreciated on decorated shelves & around nooks.

——————————————Downpourofwords

Footnote: *To be well read is a yearning almost all of humankind has on their minds yet there are only a select few who divulge passionately into the act of conscious reading, for the betterment of their lives. And in most cases, the people with a real hunger to read books do not have the financial backing to be able to own those books, except from libraries.*

The mystique

To be waiting on one's past,
Is like betting on a battered raft,
Like not being fully torn apart,
Still holding onto a weakened shaft,
Like being stuck in a desert quite far,
As a monument to visit, from the past,
With the horizons open till wide & far,
Yet nowhere to go near or far.
For since when have boats sailed over sands,
Like a life lived only fulfilling errands.
To try & recreate the past, though an act clever,
Is like joining pieces of a broken mirror,
For when looking for a way forward is what we seek,
A rejoined mirror image, would it be clear & neat?
To experience the new, is a feeling unique,
And in what memories to make, there's lies the mystique.

—————————————Downpourofwords

Footnote: *Anyone who's lives live to be an adult, has a past. And irrespective of the magnitude of the rights or the wrongs of the incidents or experiences of the past, there is usually a tendency to hang onto those memories & this can at times adversely impact one's present & the past. The poem reflects on the act of being caught up in one's past to being like a battered raft stuck in the desert sands with nowhere to go.*